Martin Thomas Lamb

Book of Mormon : Is It From God?

Lectures Delivered in the First Baptist Church, Salt Lake City, Utah

Martin Thomas Lamb

Book of Mormon : Is It From God?
Lectures Delivered in the First Baptist Church, Salt Lake City, Utah

ISBN/EAN: 9783337004934

Printed in Europe, USA, Canada, Australia, Japan

Cover: Foto ©Lupo / pixelio.de

More available books at **www.hansebooks.com**

BOOK OF MORMON:

Is it from God?

LECTURES

Delivered in the
First Baptist Church, Salt Lake City, Utah,

—BY—

Rev. ~~M.~~ T. LAMB,

And Published by Request of
HIS EXCELLENCY, GOVERNOR MURRAY,
And Others.

PRINTED FOR THE AUTHOR BY
THE SALT LAKE HERALD JOB DEPARTMENT.

1886.

➤REQUEST⁜FOR⁜PUBLICATION⬅

L 14

SALT LAKE CITY, UTAH, July 2, 1885.

Dear Sir:

The crowded houses, in attendance when your course of lectures were delivered in this city, suggest the propriety of giving to them a circulation beyond those who heard them, and giving to the general public the results of your research into the Book of Mormon.

With this end in view we request that you publish the course, in such form as may seem best.

Respectfully,

ELI H. MURRAY,	THOS. MARSHALL,
A. B. CARLTON,	JOSEPH R. WALKER,
G. L. GODFREY,	L. U. COLBATH,
ARTHUR L. THOMAS,	E. T. SPRAGUE,
G. S. ERB,	C. K. GILCHRIST,
B. G. RAYBOULD,	T. W. LINCOLN,
	ROBT. G. MCNIECE.

To the Rev. Mr. M. T. Lamb.

Rev. M. T. Lamb, Assistant Pastor First Baptist Church, Salt Lake City, Utah:

Dear Brother:

It is with great pleasure that I submit the following, being a resolution unanimously adopted by the members of the First Baptist Church, convened in a regular meeting last evening:

"Having been exceedingly interested and instructed by the lectures recently delivered by Brother Lamb, assistant pastor of this church, on the Book of Mormon, and being fully persuaded of his capability and skill in handling this important subject successfully, and to the interests of the cause of Christ,

"BE IT RESOLVED, That we, as a church, heartily unite in the request already made by His Excellency, Governor Eli H. Murray, and others, that Bro. Lamb take steps immediately to have said lectures published in order that they may be brought within the reach of all.

Yours truly,

F. W. BLOHM,
Church Clerk.

A Word of Explanation.

The preparation and delivery of the following lectures was undertaken with great diffidence and hesitation. Only one person in the city favored it. The majority of his own people were not present at the delivery of his first lecture. They had heard so much upon the various peculiarities of the Mormon Church that the subject had become nauseous, and the Mormons themselves had become so used to the sallies of their opponents that they took it as a matter of course and only smiled when a new announcement was made. After studying the situation carefully, however, the author became satisfied that he had something somewhat out of the usual beaten path, and that if honestly, earnestly and kindly presented, it would receive attention and accomplish some good. He accordingly posted a few notices in the neighborhood of his church, and advertised in the various city papers, nearly all of which kindly made a special note of the lecture.

The Sunday morning Herald, for instance, contained a local item somewhat after this fashion:

"SOMETHING NEW!

Rev. Mr. Lamb, of the Baptist church, has posted a few handbills in the neighborhood of his church, announcing a lecture upon the Book of Mormon to-night, promising 'a calm, earnest discussion, entirely free from any abuse or slander or ill will,' etc. If the gentleman succeeds in fulfilling his pledge, and can get through the entire lecture without descending to abuse or slander or exhibiting ill will, he will do better than many of the Mormon opponents, and will deserve a candid hearing, especially as he promises something new and fresh in the line of a discussion of the Mormon problem."

This notice in the Herald, probably, had mainly to do with the bringing out a large number of Mormons, who packed the house to overflowing, so that aside from the one-hundred extra chairs brought into requisition, many remained standing during the entire service.

The promise of the lecturer was so faithfully carried out that the Mormons almost universally expressed their satisfaction and pleasure and determined to hear the course through. Next Sabbath evening, the schoolroom in the rear of the main audience room was thrown open and partially seated, and almost every available inch of sitting or standing room in the entire building was occupied. And the same was repeated the third evening, multitudes going away who could not get in even at the door.

The unusual, and to the author, the altogether unexpected interest taken in the lectures during their delivery, added to the very kind request of His Excellency, Gov. Murray, and the other honorable gentlemen whose names are associated with his, backed up by the unanimous vote of his own church, is the author's only excuse for thus presenting his humble efforts to the public.

He would have been glad had time and opportunity permitted a careful and thorough review. His prayer is that in their wider field they may awaken thought, lead to investigation, and finally result in the establishment of truth.

Believing, as his intercourse with Mormon neighbors and his contact with a large number of Mormon families has led him to believe, that the majority of them are honest and sincere in their convictions, and regard the Book of Mormon as inspired of God, he feels profoundly moved as he ventures to come before them with so unwelcome a message as the word "fraud" must necessarily be. And yet, having reached this conclusion by what seems to him irresistible logic and unanswerable arguments, he dare not, as an honest and conscientious Christian man, who must answer at the bar of God for faithfulness or neglect, withhold his conclusions.

And he takes this opportunity of asking sincerely and earnestly any honest Mormon, who, after carefully weighing the arguments herein presented against the divine origin of the Book of Mormon, if he can present a real satisfactory reply, to do so through the public press, or by private correspondence, only hoping that any replies made, whether public or private, shall be made in the same kind, charitable, Christian spirit the author has, at least, tried to maintain throughout this discussion. M. T. LAMB.

SALT LAKE CITY, UTAH, JULY, 1885.

BOOK OF MORMON.

Is it from God?

LECTURE I.

"The words of the Lord are pure words; as silver tried in a furnace of earth, purified seven times."—Ps. 12, 6.

The Book of Mormon lies at the foundation, is the corner stone of the Mormon Church:

"We consider the Bible, Book of Mormon, Book of Doctrine and Covenants, Pearl of Great Price and Sayings of Joseph the Seer, our guides in faith and doctrine. The first four have been adopted as such by a vote of the saints in general conference."—From preface of "A Compendium of the Doctrines of the Gospel."

"We believe the Bible to be the word of God, as far as it is translated correctly: we also believe the Book of Mormon to be the word of God."—Art. 8 of "Articles of Faith."

A slight hint that the Book of Mormon has one great advantage over the Bible: it was translated by divine inspiration, the Bible was not. The translation of the Bible was the work of fallible men, and therefore liable to many errors; the Book of Mormon was translated through "Urim and Thummim," helped by an angel sent from heaven, and therefore free from the errors that necessarily attach to a human translation.

"And we know also that they have been translated by the gift and power of God, for his voice hath declared it unto us; wherefore we know of a certainty that the work is true."—Affidavit of "The Three Witnesses." See preface to Book of Mormon

"The tablets or plates were translated by Smith, who used a small, oval or kidney-shaped stone, called Urim and Thummim, that seemed endowed with the marvelous power of converting the characters on the plates, when used by Smith, into English, who would then dictate to Cowdry what to write."—Statement of David Whitmer. See "Myth of the Manuscript Found," p. 83.

Martin Harris "explained the translation as follows: By aid of the seer-stone, sentences would appear and were read by the prophet and written by Martin,* and when finished, he would say 'Written,' and if correctly written, that sentence would disappear and another appear in its place, but if not written correctly, it remained until corrected, so that the translation was just as it was engraven on the plates, precisely in the language then used."—Myth of the M. F., p. 91.

In addition to the very great advantage the Book of Mormon possesses over the Bible in an inspired translation, it possesses other advantages:

"If the prophetical part of this wonderful book be compared with the prophetical declarations of the Bible, there will be found much evidence in the latter to establish the truth of the former. But though there are many predictions in the Book of Mormon relating to the great events of the last days which the Bible gives us no information about, yet there is nothing in the predictions of the Bible that contradicts in the least the predictions of the Book of Mormon."

"If the doctrinal part of the Book of Mormon be compared with the doctrines of the Bible, there will be found the same perfect harmony which we find on the comparison of the prophetical parts of the two books, although there are many points of the doctrine of Christ that are far more plain and definite in the Book of Mormon than in the Bible, and many things revealed in relation to doctrine that never could be fully learned from the Bible."—"Divine Authenticity of the Book of Mormon," by Orson Pratt.

---

*Martin Harris wrote a small portion of the book only. The major portion was written by Oliver Cowdry.

The Book of Mormon is then superior to the Bible in at least three respects:

a.—It was infallibly translated.

b.—It has in it "many predictions relating to the great events of the last days which the Bible gives us no information about;" and,

c.—"There are many points of the doctrine of Christ that are far more plain and definite in the Book of Mormon than in the Bible; and many things revealed in relation to doctrine that never could be fully learned from the Bible."

And this view of the superior merits of the Book of Mormon came from a very high source—from the Prophet and Seer, Joseph Smith, himself.

"Nov. 28th, 1841.—In council with the twelve apostles, Joseph Smith said: 'I told the brethren that the Book of Mormon was the most correct of any book on earth, and the keystone of our religion, and a man would get nearer to God by abiding by its precepts than by any other book."—Compendium, p. 273.

This central place accorded the Book of Mormon by the Mormon Church is quite a sufficient excuse for asking your attention to a consideration of its claims to divine authority. The following earnest, incisive words from Orson Pratt I most heartily approve:

"This book must be either true or false. If true, it is one of the most important messages ever sent from God to man, affecting both the temporal and eternal interests of every people under heaven to the same extent and in the same degree that the message of Noah affected the inhabitants of the old world. If false, it is one of the most cunning, wicked, bold, deep-laid impositions ever palmed upon the world; calculated to deceive and ruin millions who will sincerely receive it as the word of God, and will suppose themselves securely built upon the rock of truth until they are plunged, with their families, into hopeless despair.

"The nature of the message in the Book of Mormon is such that, if true, no one can possibly be saved and reject it; if false, no one can possibly be saved and receive it. There fore, every soul in all the world is equally interested in ascertaining its truth or falsity. In a matter of such infinite importance, no person should rest satisfied with the conjectures or opinions of others. He should use every exertion himself to become acquainted with the nature of the message; he should carefully examine the evidences of which it is offered to the world; he should, with all patience and perseverence, seek to acquire a certain knowledge whether it be of God or not.

"If, after a rigid examination, it be found an imposition, it should be extensively published to the world as such. The evidence and arguments upon which the imposture was detected should be clearly and logically stated, that those who have been sincerely, yet unfortunately, deceived may perceive the nature of the deception, and be reclaimed, and that those who continue to publish the delusion may be exposed and silenced."—Introduction to "Divine Authenticity of the Book of Mormon."

This Book of Mormon, like our Bible, is made up of several books, some fifteen all together, purporting to have been written by different authors extending through a period of 1000 years, beginning 600 years before Christ and closing 400 years after Christ.*

It records the history of a small colony, embracing two families, who left the City of Jerusalem during the reign of Zedekiah, King of Judah, 600 years before Christ; wandered for a time in the Desert of Arabia, then built ships of a peculiar construction, in which they embarked and were drifted across the Indian Ocean, led by the hand of a strange Providence, until at last, crossing the Pacific, they landed on the shores of South America, where they grew into a numerous and wealthy people, and although divided into two rival factions, they continued to increase until they had spread over the greater portion of North and South America.

About 150 years before Christ, by a special revela-

---

*One book, the "Book of Ether," professes to be a compilation, by the Prophet Moroni, from twenty-four ancient plates, purporting to be the record of a people who came over to this country directly after the "Confusion of tongues," as recorded in Gen. 11, 1-9, and lived and flourished here for over 1000 years, and were then utterly exterminated.

tion from heaven, a Christian Church was organized, and the ordinance of baptism administered by immersion. Churches rapidly multiplied, and the truth continued to extend until it controlled in a measure the destinies of the whole people.

A few days after Jesus' crucifixion and resurrection in Jerusalem, as recorded in the New Testament, he appeared in person to the churches and the people on this continent; remained with them forty days, preaching the gospel, performing a multitude of strange miracles, establishing the faith of his people, &c. But after he left them there was a sad apostacy from the faith; dissensions and differences increased, wars bitter and relentless occured. Matters grew worse and worse until, in the year A. D. 384, the entire population of the two continents met in deadly conflict around the sacred hill Cumorah, and one of the most sanguinary battles that the pages of history anywhere records resulted in the complete annihilation of the one party by the destruction of their 230,000 warriors, and the closing up of the divinely inspired records, and the hiding of the plates containing the Book of Mormon, where they remained for a period of 1400 years, until Joseph Smith, by the direction of the resurrected Moroni, found their hiding place and brought them forth to the world.

On May 8, 1838, Joseph Smith, when asked, "How and where did you obtain the Book of Mormon?" gave this answer:

"Moroni, who deposited the plates (from whence the Book of Mormon was translated,) in a hill in Manchester, Ontario County, New York, being dead and raised again therefrom, appeared unto me, and told me where they were, and gave me directions how to obtain them. I obtained them, and the Urim and Thummim with them, by means of which I translated the plates. And thus came the Book of Mormon."—"Compendium," p. 305.

In inviting your attention, to-night, to a candid and careful examination of the claims of the Book of Mormon to divine inspiration, I ask, friends, first of all, that you will listen to the considerations I present with the same candor and earnest desire to know the truth that I myself have constantly sought to cherish in the preparation. It is in my nature to be charitable, to take the side of the weakest; to feel a profound sympathy for the oppressed, the maligned, the persecuted. When therefore I began the study of the Book of Mormon, I brought to it an honest desire to know the truth, and a full determination to judge it with all possible charity, and be convinced of its value, its true inspiration, if I could find any real genuine proofs that it came from God.

And yet it is due you, and but the part of candor to confess, that a long and patient study of the proofs of the divine inspiration of the Bible—a careful examination of many of the objections infidels and sceptics during the ages past have urged against it—have made me perhaps *somewhat more critical and exacting in my demands* than I otherwise might have been. I cannot accept anything as inspired of God unless the *plain marks of inspiration are found upon it.* God's finger-marks must be clearly visible.

The ground taken is this: God does not do things as men do. He stamps himself, his own infinite perfections upon everything he undertakes. He never does things by halves, never bungles or makes mistakes. Whether he creates a mountain or the tiniest insect, whether a blade of grass or a drop of water, he displays a wisdom, a skill, a perfection utterly beyond the reach of fallible, blundering, imperfect man. He makes no blunders, his finger-marks are perfection—"All his works praise him,"—and no exception to this statement is possible.

And so his finger-marks are seen, must be seen in every word he inspires. Whether he records a history, utters a prophecy, or inspires a proverb or a psalm, he does it in a way that is like himself; he stamps his own infinite nature upon it, so that the words of the psalmist are always found true: "Thy testimonies are wonderful." "Every word of God is pure," pure "as silver tried in a furnace of earth, purified seven times" language that cannot possibly be true of any merely human production. So completely is this true of the Bible, dear friends, that one rule all the best critics in the world have been forced to adopt is this: "Every book in the Bible, to be accepted as divine, must, in its style of composition, in its contents, its general make up, be such as no man on earth, or any number of men, could possibly compose."

Any book, therefore, to secure recognition and reverence as from God, should plainly reveal God's finger-marks in its every part. No awkward blundering, no stooping to slang phrases, no exhibition of human weaknesses in any direction. Every word of it that purports to come from him, every thought that expresses his thought, must be as pure as perfection itself, or it could not have come from that fountain of purity, "as silver purified seven times," until every particle of dross has been eliminated. And permit me to say, friends, every book in the Bible has a thousand times over during the ages past been subjected to this severe ordeal, and has come out of every trial "without the smell of fire" upon its fair pages.

If then, the Book of Mormon, upon a candid and careful examination shall be able to pass this searching test; if its style of composition is such that no man on earth could have produced it; if its contents continually breathe the atmosphere of the Infinite One—the pure and holy God; if there is nothing foolish in it, no mistakes, no exhibition of the common weaknesses and frailties of our poor, weak, perverted human natures; if, when it is carefully dissected, as one would dissect, with a microscope, a blade of grass, or a drop of water, or a grain of sand, a wonderful completion and perfection is everywhere displayed, then I shall be bound to accept the Book of Mormon, as I am bound for the same reason to accept every book in this Book of Books as the direct offspring of God himself. Let me then, tonight, very briefly call your attention to one strange peculiarity of the Bible that stamps it as divine, and then briefly examine the Book of Mormon to see whether it exhibits the same marks of the divine hand.

Suppose you pick up a blade of grass or a kernel of wheat, or a simple hair, falling from the head, or a single drop of water, and look at it. At first you will say "What of it? I see nothing strange, nothing divine in this little affair." But begin carefully to study it. Take your microscope and dissect it, and you shall be astonished at the revelations made. Almost a thousand evidences of the handiwork of God, as completely beyond the wisdom and skill and power of men as is the creation of a world. So, if you please, turn at random to any one of the short historical incidents found in the Bible, and read it over. At first reading, you may notice nothing at all peculiar about it. Its plain, simple, nothing constrained or studied, no effort at crispness or sharpness, or condensation; no attempt at oratorical or rhetorical display, no embellishments of any kind. A simple, straightforward, matter of fact statement. And you say, "There's nothing strange about that. Any one could write after that fashion." But wait a little. Study this little incident carefully, and presently you will begin to discern some strange things about it.

I have read the life of Washington, the father of our country—presume I have read enough about him to fill a good sized volume; possibly several volumes. In the Bible I have read a few short statements about the Patriarch Abraham. Probably not over four or five pages, all told, tell us all we knew about Abraham. And yet if called upon to describe the characters of the two men I should feel more at home with Abraham than Washington; seem better acquainted, really know more of him, and why? Because in those few incidents of Bible history is a better, more complete and comprehensive delineation of character than in all the volumes written about Washington.

Try an experiment: Procure a correct history of the United States, and read the long chapter of fifty pages that describes the traitorous plot of Arnold when he sought to deliver a division of our army into the hands of the British. Then take your New Testament and read the ten or dozen verses that tell us all we know of the traitor Judas Iscariot, and when done see if you do not feel better acquainted with the true character of Judas, really knew more about him than about Arnold.

Read carefully through a well written life of Napoleon Bonaparte; occupy a week, or a month if necessary, in a careful study of the man, his character and moral worth. Then turn to 2nd Chron., 28 chapter, and read twenty verses about King Ahaz and his people. Spend one or two hours only in reading and rereading, and then take up your pen and see which of the two you can write about with the greatest clearness and definiteness. A few such experiments as this will satisfy you that there is a wonderful difference between the Bible and every other book in this respect. A few verses will draw out a man's character to the very life, proving the assertion of the Apostle true: "The word of God is quick and powerful, sharper than any two edged sword, piercing even to the dividing asunder of soul and spirit, * * * and is a discerner of the thoughts and intents of the heart."

As the skillful artist will sometimes, by a few master-strokes of his brush, produce a picture that seems almost to live and breathe before you, so a few master-strokes from God's pen will probe to the bottom of the human heart, unmask the moral character, and hold it up naked and uncovered where all the world can behold it.

But the same wonderful peculiarity can be seen in other things besides description of character. The histories furnished are just so concise and comprehensive. A single verse often will tell of a long and bloody battle. The transactions of a whole campaign are crowded into a few sentences. And yet the discription is simplicity itself—not the least appearance of crowding, no seeming effort at condensation or brevity. There is nothing that can at all equal this in the history of man. Imagine a poor cripple made whole by a miracle. Take pen and paper and attempt a discription. Give a touching account of the poor cripple's previous history, the time and place of the occurrence; describe all the circumstances attending the miracle, who performed it, how it was done, what people thought of it, and how the cripple was affected by it. Describe the whole in as few words as possible, without copying from the Bible, and if you compress your story into five or six pages you will do remarkably well. But in the New Testament such a scene is fully and completely described in five short verses.

The life and character and times of the most remarkable and important personage that has ever appeared on earth, the Lord Jesus Christ, is, by Matthew beautifully and clearly exhibited in the small compass of thirty-one pages print. And be it remembered, Matthew was an unlettered man, not at all used to writing. This book, his first and last attempt, so far as we know. But Washington Irving was one of the most learned and excellent writers the world has ever seen—had practiced writing and the art of condensing all his life, and yet he could not exhibit the life and character and times of George Washington short of five or six octavo volumes.

D'Aubeigne has written the history of the great reformation in Germany in *five* large volumes. Luke, in the Acts of the Apostles, has furnished us the history of quite as extensive a reformation in *thirty-three pages*. And in fact, friends, this wonderful comprehensiveness, this strange tact at compression, this unapproachable ability to say a great deal in a few words, prevails all through the Bible. It's one of God's finger-marks— precisely what we might expect from a being of infinite perfections. Why, dear friends, I can safely challenge all the doctors of divinity, or skilled writers of the present age, to crowd into *ten pages* every thought and sentiment and inference. the Apostle Paul, with the greatest grace and simplicity, puts into one page.

A young man in old Dr. Wayland's class, once flippantly remarked about the Proverbs of Solomon, which they happened to be studying: "Why it's easy enough to write *proverbs*; anybody could do that." The Doctor simply replied: "Try a few."

Try your hand, friends, at writing history, or biography, or doctrine, or parable, or proverb, and place your production along side of God's; and I'll abide the result, yourself being the judge. One of our poets has sung:

> "Let all the heathen writers join
> To form one perfect book:
> Great God, when once compared with thine,
> How mean their writings look!"

Look at the discourses of our Lord, any one of them —the Lord's prayer, if you please; or the whole Sermon on the Mount. Surely "never man spake like this man." The first eight sentences of that sermon on the mount are by universal consent placed above any other eight sentences ever spoken by mortal lips. Friend and foe, infidel, atheist and christian, have from the first acknowledged that these verses stand alone amid all the literature of earth, unapproached and unapproachable, not more in their comprehensiveness and sublimity than in their beautiful simplicity:

> "Blessed are the poor in spirit, for theirs is the kingdom of heaven.
> "Blessed are the meek, for they shall inherit the earth.
> "Blessed are they that hunger and thirst after righteousness, for they shall be filled.
> "Blessed are the merciful, for they shall obtain mercy.
> "Blessed are the pure in heart, for they shall see God," &c., &c.

And, please reflect, that sermon was an extemporaneous, impromptu discourse, and the first extended sermon, so far as we know, preached by the man Christ Jesus—a young man, only thirty years old, who had never been in the schools, not even in the common schools; never studied the art of composition, or practiced compression. But he opens his mouth, and from his lips flow words so divine, both in the thought and in the style of expression, that they have never been approached by mortal man. And the wonder is only increased when we reflect, it is the pen of Matthew the publican that records this sermon, some *twenty-five or thirty years after it was preached.* If Matthew remembered the exact words of the Savior, and wrote just as first spoken, it was a wonderful *miracle of memory.* If he only remembered the substance of the sermon, and clothed Jesus' thought in his own language, then we have a still greater miracle to account for:—an *ignorant, unlettered publican, almost infinitely outstripping all the skilled writers on earth!*

It would be easy to multiply illustrations of this thought, for the whole Bible in its every part is an illustration. In fact, friends, if any portion of the Bible, any book in it, should fail to exhibit clearly and truly these necessary and reasonable credentials of the divine hand, it would be reason enough for rejecting it and denying it a place in the scriptures of truth; for, according to the test of our text, all the words of the Lord should be "pure words;" as "silver tried in a furnace of earth, purified seven times."

And now, let us very briefly, and yet carefully and honestly, apply this test of divinity to the Book of Mormon.

The time is so limited that we shall be able to examine only two or three brief specimens to night. But, the subject will be continued, for I do not design to allow even the suspicion of *unfairness* in the selection of specimens.

I opened the Book of Mormon at random the other day, to the 110th page and read from 2nd Nephi, 14, 10, the following sentences:

"And now I, Nephi, must make an end of my prophesying unto you, my beloved brethren. And I cannot write but a few things, which I know must surely come to pass. Wherefore, the things which I have written sufficeth me, save it be a few words which I must speak concerning the doctrine of Christ; wherefore, I shall speak unto you plainly, according to the plainness of my prophesying."

Have read you sixty-nine words.

And, now, friends, I am not gifted at all in the art of condensing—have had very little practice or culture in that direction. Multitudes of writers can easily "beat me by half." In the present case, I have used the author's words almost exclusively, simply leaving out the inelegant and uncalled for repetitions, the unnecessary verbiage, &c., and yet preserving every thought of the writer in a much simpler, neater, and better constructed sentence of only thirty-two words, as follows:

"And now I, Nephi, must close my prophesying, with a few words plainly spoken, according to my custom, concerning the doctrine of Christ; words which I know must surely come to pass."

I turn again to page 318 and read from Book of Alma, 19, 4-5:

"Now, I unfold unto you a mystery; nevertheless, there are many mysteries which are kept that no one knoweth them, save God himself. But I show unto you one thing, which I have inquired diligently of God, that I might know, that is concerning the resurrection. Behold, there is a time appointed that all shall come forth from the dead. Now, when this time cometh, no one knows; but God knoweth the time which is appointed. Now, whether there shall be one time, or a second time, or a third time, that men shall come forth from the dead, it mattereth not, for God knoweth all these things; and it sufficeth me to know that this is the case; that there is a time appointed that all shall rise from the dead. Now, there must needs be a space betwix the time of death, and the time of the resurrection.

And now I would enquire what becometh of the souls of men from this time of death to the time appointed for the resurrection? Now, whether there is more than one time appointed for man to rise, it mattereth not; for all do not die at once : and this mattereth not ; all is as one day with God, and time only is measured unto men ; therefore, there is a time appointed unto men that they shall rise from the dead; and there is a space between the time of death and the resurrection. And now concerning this space of time, what becometh of the souls of men is the thing which I have enquired dilligently of the Lord to know; and this is the thing of which I do know; And when the time cometh when all shall rise, then shall they know that God knoweth all the times which are appointed unto men. Now, concerning the state of the soul between death and the resurrection: Behold, it has been made known unto me, by an angel, that the spirits of all men, as soon as they are departed from the mortal body, yea, the spirits of all men, whether they be good or evil, are taken home to that God who gave them life."

Have read you in all 365 words.

Now, please carefully observe that I include every thought and even hint of the author, and yet condense into 142 words everything he has said in 365 words:

"There are many mysteries, which only God may know; but, having inquired diligently of him, he permits me to unfold unto you a mystery concerning the resurrection. Behold, there is a time appointed, known only to God, when all shall come forth from the dead ; whether all at the same time, or at differnt times, it does not matter, God knows and that is sufficient ; all do not die at once ; time is measured unto man, but with God all is as one day. And when the resurrection cometh, then all shall know that God knoweth all the times which are appointed unto man.

"Behold, it has been made known unto me by an angel, that the spirits of all men, as soon as they are departed from this mortal body, whether good or evil, are taken home to that God who gave them life."

These are still awkwardly expressed sentences. If we should ignore the author's language and his unnatural arrangement, treating of the resurrection *before* he treats of the intermediate state, we might put his thoughts in a still briefer compass, somewhat as follows:

"There are many mysteries known only to God ; but, having earnestly asked him, he has revealed to me through an angel, the following glorious facts:

"First—that the spirits of all men, good and evil,

when they depart from this mortal body, are immediately taken home to the God who gave them life.

"Second— as to the time of the final resurrection from the dead, it is not known to us whether all are to be raised at the same time, or at different times; but, when it finally occurs, then we shall know that God knew all about it."

This, as you can readily see, is the substance of the above immense revelation that required the help of an angel of God ; and that occupies nearly a full page of the Book of Mormon.

Once more, let me read you a sentence upon page 224, Book of Alma, 3, 7.

"And now I say unto you, that this is the order after which I am called: yea, to preach unto my beloved brethren; yea, and every one that dwelleth in the land; yea, to preach unto all, both old and young, both bond and free: yea, I say unto you the aged, and also the middle aged, and the rising generation; yea, to cry unto them that they must repent and be born again; yea, thus saith the spirit, repent, all ye ends of the earth, for the kingdom of heaven is soon at hand; yea, the Son of God cometh in his glory, in his might majesty, power and dominion. Yea, my beloved brethren, I say unto you, that the spirit saith, behold the glory of the king of all the earth; and also the king of heaven shall very soon shine forth among all the children of men: and also the spirit saith unto me, yea, crieth unto me with a mighty voice, saying, go forth and say unto this people, repent, for except ye repent ye can in nowise inherit the kingdom of heaven."

I ask you, friends, what has the author said in all these 187 words? Only this:—

"I am commissioned by the spirit, speaking in thunder tones, to preach repentance to my brethren, and to all the people of the land, because the kingdom of heaven is at hand, when the Son of God, king of earth and heaven, cometh in majesty and glory." Forty-seven instead of 187 words.

It has been suggested that the blunders in composition, awkward and uncalled for repetitions, sentences constructed in defiance of all rhetorical rules, often covering up and obscuring the thought of the author, must all be explained by the fact that Joseph Smith was an uneducated and unlettered youth.

But, please reflect a moment. These sentences are, professedly, a translation of an ancient record—transfering to our language words and thoughts already written in an ancient tongue. In such a translation the *translator*, if he is a poor English scholar, may *misspell* the words of our language; he may easily make grammatical mistakes in the construction of his sentences; may use unnecessary words in the expression of a single thought; but, he may not repeat a thought three or four times over, as in the above examples, *except those repetitions are found in the original, from which he is translating*. For instance, in the last quotation:

"And now I say unto you, that this is the order after which I am called; yea, to preach unto my beloved brethren; yea, and every one that dwelleth in the land."

It is evident there must have been something engraven upon those ancient plates containing this idea—that he was commissioned to preach to all his brethren, and to every person dwelling in the land.

But then, there must have been added to this first statement something in those ancient plates that involved this further statement:

"Yea, to preach unto all, both old and young, both bond and free;"

or else Joseph Smith added it without authority, and thus trifled with his readers. And the same is true of the third clause, or repetition:

"Yea, I say unto you the aged, and also the middle aged, and the rising generation."

Either these repetitions were found upon those original plates, or they were added by Joseph Smith to the translation. If they were added by Mr. Smith, then he has trifled with sacred things, committed the fearful sin of adding to the words of divine revelation; loading down God's pure words with so much useless rubbish as to cast doubt and discredit upon the whole. And, if he could or would do this in these instances, what warrant have we that he has not *frequently* done it? in fact, that the whole book has not been thus altered or embellished to suit his own fancies?

But, the facts are, Joseph Smith did not, himself translate a single sentence. The statements of the eye-witnesses are very plain upon this point:

> "And we know, also, that they have been translated by the gift and power of God."—The "Three Witnesses."
>
> "The tablets, or plates were translated by Smith, who used a small oval, or kidney-shaped stone, called Urim and Thummim, that seemed endowed with the marvelous power of converting the characters on the plates, when used by Smith, into English."—David Whitmer.
>
> "By aid of the seer-stone, sentences would appear and were read by the prophet * * * so that the translation was just as it was engraven on the plates, precisely in the language then used."—Martin Harris.

It is plain from these statements that Joseph Smith had no responsibility whatever as to the wording of the translation. The stone itself was endowed "by the gift of God" with the "marvelous power of converting the characters on the plates into English." The English "sentences would appear on the stone and were read by the prophet." All Mr. Smith had to do, then, was simply to read what appeared on the stone.

We are forced therefore to the conclusion that all these senseless repetitions, this worse than useless verbiage, *is and must have been in the original plates, and not at all the result of Mr. Smith's ignorance and want of culture.*

And hence we must call in question the divine inspiration of those original plates, inasmuch as such blundering repetitions are directly at variance with all we have learned of God's style of writing.

If it be said, by way of excuse for such sins against all the ordinary rules of composition, that the authors of those old sentences I have read you, Nephi and Alma, may have been unlettered men, I reply, first: These men were not unlettered men. Nephi claims to have been taught "in all the learning" of his father, and both of them were the leading men, the best posted men of their times. I reply, second: Even if they had been unlettered men, they could not have made such blunders had they been inspired of God. Matthew, the publican, author of the Gospel of Matthew, was an unletrered man. Peter and James, authors of three epistles, were unlettered men. John, author of one of the Gospels, the Book of Revelation, and three brief epistles, was an unlettered man, and so was the Lord Jesus himself an unlettered man. But where in all their writings or speeches can you find any such egregious blunders in composition as these specimens from the Book of Mormon? On the contrary, under the inspiration of the Holy Spirit, they made most wonderful use of the Greek language, as we have already learned, exhibiting a style so terse and making choice of words so comprehensive, that they have never been approached by the most skillful writers on earth.

So far then, friends, our examination is absolutely against the inspiration of the Book of Mormon.

The specimens examined reveal no divine fingermarks—they only equal the blundering efforts of unlettered men. But we have only examined three brief specimens; these may prove peculiar exceptions. We will see in our next.

LECTURE II.

"For my thoughts are not your thoughts, neither are your ways my ways, saith the Lord.

"For as the heavens are higher than the earth, so are my ways higher than your ways, and my thoughts than your thoughts." Isaiah 55: 8, 9.

I desire at the beginning of the lecture this evening to make plain and prominent the thought presented last Sabbath evening, that the Book of Mormon must be judged by the same tests of divinity as are applied, and have, during the ages past, been applied to the Bible. .It must bear the same clear impress of the divine hand upon its pages, or we cannot accept it as from God.

Last Sabbath evening the Bible was examined as to its style of composition, its peculiar way of saying things. There was found a remarkable terseness and comprehensiveness. It says a great deal in a few words. In its delineations of character, it is especially so. A few strokes rom its master pen will lay open the human heart to its core, giving us clearer and juster views of a man's real character than any human writer has ever been able to express with ten times the number of words.

The same strange tact at compression, ability to say a great deal in a few words, and yet saying it with wonderful simplicity and grace, are found in the historical narratives of the Bible. Various illustrations of this were given; and, then, specimen passages were read from the Book of Mormon that not only failed utterly to come up to the divine standard of terseness and comprehensiveness of statement, but that, judged even by ordinary human standards, exhibited a looseness, a verbosity, a reckless disregard of the simplest rules of composition, would hardly be tolerated in a common school boy. The first passage, containing sixty-nine words, was easily compressed into a sentence of thirty-two words. The second passage, containing 365 words, had 228 words left out of it, without the loss of a single thought, and with the advantage of a clearer and more vigorous presentation of the thoughts of the author, while the substance of the passage was presented in a still briefer form. The third passage, containing 187 words, was easily boiled down into a sentence containing forty-seven words, or one fourth the number in the book.

But, not wishing to judge the whole book by two or three brief specimens hastily selected, it was proposed to continue the examination this evening with a selection, covering such a broad range as to give us a fair idea of the prevailing style of the entire book.

However, to make the examination as complete and valuable as possible, and taking for granted there are many here to night who were not here last Sabbath, it is proposed, first, to spend a little time in still further illustrating God's strange tact at compression, his peculiar way of saying a great deal in a few words, by calling your attention to a specimen recorded in the seventh chapter of the book of Daniel.

In a vision by night, the prophet Daniel was caused to see *four great beasts* come out of the sea, diverse one from the other. And, in the explanation of the vision, given in the latter part of the same chapter, we are informed that these four beasts were designed to represent four different kingdoms that were to arise, one after the other. First, the Chaldean, or Babylonian; second, the Persian, or Medo-Persian; third, the Macedonian; and fourth, the Roman.

At the time this vision was seen by Daniel, the first of these four kingdoms, the Babylonian, was in the height of her glory and power. She stood at the head of all the nations of the earth: from her majesty and beauty and power she was called, "The lady of kingdoms, the beauty of the Chaldees excellency, and the glory of the whole earth." She attained her position and eminence chiefly through the energy and skill of her greatest king, Nebuchadnezzar. With great rapidity he subdued the nations about him, pushing his conquests onward until proud Tyre fell, Jerusalem was taken and destroyed, and Egypt became a tributary province; and no nation was found to dispute his sway.

But the riches and luxury and glory brought into Babylon by Nebuchadnezzar became the means of destruction to his successors. They became effeminate and weak; no troubles from without to call forth the energies and power of the nation; king, princes and people gave themselves to ease and indulgence—the enjoyment of their luxuries. And, so effeminate had they become that, when Cyrus, king of Persia, marched against Babylon, they were cowed down and affrighted, and shut themselves up closely within the walls of their great city: and, during the whole siege of two years, dare not venture out and risk a battle with the army of Cyrus.

Now, to some, it may not appear at all singular or

strange that all this history could be *fully and completely expressed in one short verse*. But, such is the fact. The first beast that came up out of the river, representing the Babylonian monarchy, is thus described by Daniel, in the fourth verse:

"The first was like a lion, and had eagle's wings; I beheld till the wings thereof were plucked and it was lifted up from the earth, and made stand upon the feet as a man, and a man's heart was given to it."

Note the facts brought out in this verse:

First—the Babylonian monarchy is compared to a *lion*. The lion is the king of all wild beasts, the most majestic, noble, powerful of the whole. Such was Babylon under Nebuchadnezzar, the first, noblest, strongest of the nations. But,

Second—it says, the lion had *eagle's wings*. The lion is itself a beast of prey, representing the fact of history that Babylon was given to making conquests, subsisting upon and plundering the nations about her. But, this was not enough, the lion had wings to show that the conquests of Nebuchadnezzar were *more rapid than ordinary*. He almost *flew* from one conquest to another.

But, says Daniel, "I beheld till the wings thereof were plucked, and it was lifted from the earth, and made stand upon the feet as a man, and a man's heart was given to it." As we have learned, after Nebuchadnezzar, the Babylonian monarchy, ceased its conquests, and its power began to wane. "Its wings were plucked." Not only so, there was eventually such a complete change that its desires for conquest were all gone, and it became so effeminate, and so much given to indulgence that a ravenous beast of prey would no longer fitly represent its character. Hence Daniel saw the lion lifted up and changed so completely in its nature that a *man's heart* was given to it.

"The first was like a lion, and had eagle's wings: I beheld till the wings thereof were plucked, and it was lifted up from the earth, and made stand upon the feet as a man, and a man's heart was given to it."

Who could imagine that so much correct history could be crowded into one short verse? But, friends, you can find a great many such wonders in the Bible; it is God's way of writing.

The next verse, the fifth, is equally remarkable:

"And behold another beast, a second, like to a bear; and it raised up itself on one side, and it had three ribs in the mouth of it, between the teeth of it; and they said thus unto it, arise, devour much flesh."

This second beast represents the Persian monarchy, and is likened to a bear, not a lion as the first. The bear has less strength, less majesty, but is no less ravenous than the lion. Such was the Persian monarchy. After the lion, or Babylonian monarchy, had lost its lion nature and been given a man's heart, it fell an easy prey to the ravenous bear, the Persians. But, it says, the bear "raised up itself on one side." This refers to the historical fact, very peculiar, but no less exactly true, that the Persians made conquests *only on one side of them.* History informs us that Cyrus and his successors never penetrated eastward of their own boundaries. The countries they subdued all lay to the west of Persia. That is west of a north and south line, but never east.

Further, the bear had "three ribs in its mouth between its teeth," showing not only its ravenous character, but exhibiting proof that it had found prey and had devoured it. The Persians, under Cyrus and his successors, succeeded in making very extensive conquests westward. Lydia, Chaldea and Egypt, and other smaller nations, were devoured, plundered of their wealth and left bare like bones. And these conquests only stirred up their hearts to attempt still greater conquests. Hence, the ribs in the bear's mouth are represented as saying, "arise, devour much flesh."

It is interesting to read the history of the Persian kings and see how exactly this bear represents their character; and especially how literally the last phrase in this short verse, "arise, devour much flesh," has been fulfilled. Cyrus was almost constantly in war until his death, which occurred on the battle field while engaged with a wild horde of barbarians, living to the northwest of Persia, about the Caspian Sea.

Cambyses his son, called in the Scriptures Artaxerxes, was still more ambitious of conquest, and far more cruel. He came into Egypt with a great army and completely destroyed it; laid much of the land desolate, and utterly ruined some of their largest and most magnificent cities. After ruining Egypt, he carried his wars into Ethiopia and Lydia, then back into Syria.

Darius, who followed him, supposed to be Ahasuerus of the book of Esther, was even more ambitious and anxious to be considered a hero, and obtain universal dominion. He marched a numerous army far into the interior of Europe, and attempted in several engagements to subdue the Greeks. But failing to accomplish his purpose, he was so exasperated that he returned home and began the most extensive preparations probably ever made for war. For three years all Asia west of the Tigris river was in commotion and busy with preparations for his great expedition, when death put an end to his labors, yet not an end to his plans and designs, for his son, Xerxes, continued the same preparations for five years more, and then marched into Greecia with the largest army, it is believed, ever collected together. The common account is, that it consisted of three million soldiers, with attendants, servants, women, etc., swelling the number to almost *five millions !*

Thus was Persia, headed by her kings, a great "bear which lifted up itself on one side, and had ribs in its mouth between its teeth, which encouraged it to arise, devour much flesh."

But, in the sixth verse, we have a brief outline of the third nation or kingdom that came into power: the Macedonian, under Alexander the Great.

"After this I beheld, and lo another like a leopard, which had upon the back of it four wings of a fowl; the beast had also four heads; and dominion was given to it."

This verse is short, but it tells a great deal of history. First, it says, "After this," that is, after the vision of the bear: and, according to history, the Macedonian empire began its conquests about 200 years after the Persian, under Cyrus. Second, this third kingdom is compared to a leopard. The leopard, like the lion and the bear, is a beast of prey, but differs widely from them in its characteristic traits. It belongs, as is well known, to the feline, or cat tribe of animals, and very much resembles the wild cat in its disposition. It is fierce and cruel, but is especially remarkable for its *fleetness* and its peculiar manner of watching, like the cat, for its prey, and springing out upon it when it is least aware of danger.

Nothing could better express the difference between Alexander's army and the Persian than by comparing the one to a *leopard* and the other to a *bear*. The bear is heavy, clumsy and slow, the leopard light, agile and swift of foot. A single fact will sufficiently illustrate this difference. Alexander's army, when he came into Persia, consisted of only forty thousand infantry and seven thousand cavalry. And yet, so active and rapid was he, that with this small army he conquered all the then known world. The king of Persia came out against him with an army of *one million* infantry and forty thousand cavalry; but his army was completely routed, and all Persia fell into Alexander's hands.*

But, observe again, this leopard had "upon the back of it four wings of a fowl." Not enough to compare Alexander's army to one of the fleetest, most active and crafty of wild beasts, but it must have four wings to assist it in darting upon its prey, and in flying from one conquest to another. The lion had *two wings*, but this beast had *four*. Nebuchadnezzar's rapid conquests were nothing to be compared with Alexander's. The world has never seen his like before or since. Julius Cæsar, of ancient Rome, and Napoleon Bonaparte, of modern France, are the only two characters the world has ever produced who can at all bear a comparison to Alexander as a rapid conqueror. In six years time he subdued all Asia Minor, Syria, Egypt, Ethiopia, Libya, Arabia, the vast empire of Persia; had marched his victorious army into India, penetrated even beyond the Ganges, until there was not a nation known in the world that refused to acknowledge his sway.

But notice again, it says, the leopard had "four heads." Alexander died in the city of Babylon at the early age of thirty-one years, and his vast dominions descended not to his posterity, but were divided among his four chief generals.

Selucus Nicanor had Persia and the East. Perdicas, and after him Antigonus, had Asia Minor. Cassander had Macedonia; and Ptolemaus had Egypt. And these four great empires remained much the same until all were conquered by the Romans. "And dominion was given to it."

Is it not wonderful that God could cause Daniel to exhibit so much future important history in a verse no longer than this:

"After this I beheld, and lo another like a leopard, which had upon the back of it four wings of a fowl; the beast had also four heads, and dominion was given to it."

The next beast, the *fourth*, was still more wonderful; it was "dreadful and terrible and strong exceedingly." It had iron teeth and nails of brass, and break in pieces and trampled under foot the whole earth.

But pardon me, friends, for trespassing so long in presenting these specimens of God's peculiar style of writing. I desire to convince you thoroughly, and beyond the possibility of a question that God's way of putting things differs in a remarkable degree from ours, proving true the text, "My thoughts are not your thoughts, neither are your ways my ways, saith the Lord; for as the heavens are higher than the earth so are my ways higher than your ways, and my thoughts than your thoughts."

And please bear in mind, friends, that we often loose much of the energy and pith of the original by the poverty of our language to exactly express it; or perhaps I should say, by the poverty or want of skill on the part of our translators to choose the right words to fully express the divine thought of the original. For instance, the third verse of the first chapter of Genesis reads, in our English version, "And God said, let there be light, and there was light." This is short, expressive, wonderfully comprehensive; but, the Hebrew original has much more life and energy and pith. "And God said, light be!" addressing light directly in the *imperative mood*, commanding it to come forth out of the darkness. "Light be, and light was;" the light obeyed the command of her sovereign and came into being. My attention was called the past week, in one of our religious papers, to a passage in Genesis, 49: 19, which reads in our version, "Gad, a troop shall overcome him, but he shall overcome at the last." Thirteen words very brief and comprehensive. But in the original Hebrew there are only *six words*. The word Gad itself means a *troop* or *trooper;* and the phrase, "shall overcome him," is the Hebrew verb from the same word "*troop*;" and so a literal rendering would be, "Trooper, a troop troops him, but he troops last." So very comprehensive and full of pith and energy and life is the original Hebrew in which all the Old Testament was written. In the verses we have been considering, Daniel's vision, I find the first verse mentioned contains in our translation *forty-three words*; but, in the Hebrew, there are only *twenty-one* words.

Now, if we had been favored with an *inspired translation* of our Bible, if the same divine mind that first dictated these terse and vigorous and wonderfully comprehensive words had also dictated the translation, giving us the benefit of his infinite skill in the choice of words and phrases in our language best adapted to express the exact thought of the original, what a remarkable book this, our Bible, would be! Every word chosen in infinite wisdom; every phrase and sentence an exact reflection of God's thought!

Well, now, if I understand it, this is precisely what our friends claim for the Book of Mormon. Both the original composition and the translation were under the constant direction of the Holy Spirit. We have a right, therefore, have we not? to expect and demand a remarkable book; a book whose every sentence shall reveal in the most unmistakable manner the divine finger marks.

With this, therefore, in mind, let us turn to the Book of Mormon and read a few selections. It scarcely matters where we open the book. Here, for instance, is a selection from a sermon, or address of king Benjamin, one of the most earnest and devout characters appearing in the book, who declares, too, that the things "which I shall tell you *are made known unto me by an angel from God.*"—Page 150. And again, next page, "And now I have spoken the words which the Lord God·hath commanded me;" and, still again repeated, "It came to pass when king Benjamin had made an end of speaking *the words which had been delivered unto him by the angel of the Lord.*" With this very clear and oft repeated claim to inspiration, even to the selection of the words he uses, let me read you a few sentences, Book of Mosiah, 2: 2:

"And king Benjamin again opened his mouth, and began to speak unto them, saying, my friends and my brethren, my kindred and my people, I would again call your attention, that ye may hear and understand the remainder of my words which I shall speak unto you; for behold, if the knowledge of the goodness of God at this time has awakened you to a sense of your nothingness, and your worthless and fallen state;"—

As I read, I desire you will constantly challenge each statement or sentence with this question: What is there about this sentence that requires extraordinary help from God. It is good, perhaps very good, but did the author need any special help from an angel to say it?

"I say unto you, if ye have come to a knowledge of the goodness of God, and his matchless power, and his wisdom, and his patience, and his long suffering towards the children of men, and also, the atonement which has been prepared from the foundation of the world, that thereby salvation might come to him that put his trust in the Lord, and should be diligent in keeping his commandments, and continue in the faith even unto the end of his life; I mean the life of the mortal body; I say, that this is the man who receiveth salvation, through the atonement which was prepared from the foundation of the world for all mankind, which ever were, ever since the fall of Adam, or who are or who ever shall be, even unto the end of the world; and this is the means whereby salvation cometh. And there is none other salvation save this which hath been spoken of; neither are there any conditions whereby man can be saved, except the conditions which I have told you."

I ask again, friends, did the author need any special help from God to say any part of the above? Have you not heard preachers, by the hundred, in your day talk just like that, and, too, without any special assistance from an angel?

"And again I say unto you as I have said before, that as ye have come to the knowledge of the glory of God, or if ye have known of his goodness, and have tasted of his love, and have received a remission of your sins, which causeth such exceeding great joy in your souls, even so I would that ye should remember, and always retain in remembrance the greatness of God, and your own nothingness, and his goodness and long suffering towards you, unworthy creatures, and humble yourselves in the depths of humility, calling on the name of the Lord daily, and standing steadfast in the faith of that which is to come, which was spoken by the mouth of the angel; and behold, I say unto you, that if ye do this, ye shall always retain a remission of your sins; and ye shall grow in the knowledge of the glory of him that created you, or in the knowledge of that which is just and true.

"And again it is expedient that he should be diligent, that thereby he might win the prize; therefore, all things must be done in order. And I would that ye should remember, that whosoever among you borroweth of his neighbor, should return the thing that he borroweth, according as he doth agree, or else thou shalt commit sin, and perhaps thou shalt cause thy neighbor to commit sin also. And finally, I cannot tell you all the things whereby ye may commit sin; for there are divers ways and means, even so many that I cannot number them."—Sections 3 and 5.

Can you explain, friends, how God's help could be required in saying that? It is good practical sense, the most of it, though expressed in homely phrase and in loosely constructed sentences that any person in this congregation could at least equal without any help whatever from an angel of God.

But now, in contrast with this, please turn back and read with me on page 94, Second Nephi, 10: 7, a quotation from the prophet Isaiah in our Bible:

"Rejoice not thou, whole Palestina, because the rod of him that smote thee is broken, for out of the serpent's root shall come forth a cocatrice, and his fruit shall be a fiery flying serpent."

You have to stop at once; cannot take it all in at a superficial reading. Careful study is required. What do these expressions mean? Who or what is meant by the "serpent's root?" And how from such parentage can there come forth a cocatrice? And by what law of hereditary or natural selection shall the fruitage of the cocatrice be a "fiery flying serpent?" These words are evidently chosen, like Daniel's beasts, to represent character, human character and human action, and human destiny. A chance for study, surely. No human intellect is sharp enough and comprehensive enough to take in the full meaning of this one sentence at a single reading.

And the same is true of the balance of the paragraph:

"And the first born of the poor shall feed, and the needy shall lie down in safety; and I will kill the root with famine, and he shall slay thy remnant. Howl, O gate; cry, O city;

thou, whole Palestina, art dissolved: for there shall come from the north a smoke, and none shall be alone in his appointed times "

Do you notice any loosely constructed sentences, any useless verbiage in the above paragraph?

Perhaps you say this a *peculiar* passage, hard to understand. Then turn back to an easy one, page 71, Second Nephi, 5: 11, also quoted from Isaiah the prophet:

Awake, awake, put on thy strength, O Zion; put on thy beautiful garments, O Jerusalem, the holy city, for henceforth there shall no more come into thee, the uncircumcised and the unclean. Shake thyself from the dust; arise, sit down, O Jerusalem; loose thyself from the bonds of thy neck, O captive daughter of Zion."

Now, while it is apparently easy to understand this, for a rich thought lies right upon the surface, yet, when you attempt to tell *what* it means, and *all* it means, how *it grows upon you!* How *immense* it becomes! It proves a rich mine of thought, the deeper down you dig the richer it becomes and the more of it.

Take a still simpler and plainer passage, the First Psalm:

"Blessed is the man that walketh not in the council of the ungodly, nor standeth in the way of sinners, nor sitteth in the seat of the scornful.

"But his delight is in the law of the Lord, and in his law doth he meditate day and night.

"And he shall be like a tree planted by the rivers of water, that bringeth forth his fruit in his season; his leaf also shall not wither, and whatsoever he doeth shall prosper.

"The ungodly are not so, but are like the chaff which the wind driveth away."

Friends, is it not easy enough to see, that though so plain and simple, yet a volume of meaning is crowded into these words? Every verse is a text, from which a valuable sermon could easily be preached. No awkward, blundering sentences; no superficial, unnecessary roundabout phrases that require an apology for their existence. Every sentence "strikes oil;" every word has a meaning and is needed; every statement has "a volume" in it.

If you turn over to the New Testament, what could be plainer or simpler, or more beautifully expressed than Christ's sermon on the mount? And yet you have to stop at every sentence, not because it is difficult to understand, but because you discover a mine of gold in it that is not exhausted by a few moments, or even a few hours study and research. And the same thing is true of all his sermons and addresses and parables. What can equal in sublimity and beauty and pathos, and yet in real simplicity and naturalness, the Fifteenth Chapter of Luke, containing the parables of the lost sheep, the lost piece of money and the prodigal son? An inexhaustible storehouse of wealth, that all the study of the ages has neither diminished nor rendered stale.

Read over Jesus' incomparable address to his disciples, on the eve of his apprehension and crucifixion, as recorded in the Fourteenth, Fifteenth and Sixteenth Chapters of John. Every sentence has the stamp of divinity upon it. Spoken by lips that "spake as never man spake." Dissect carefully that address, and find anywhere in it the word, or the phrase, or the sentence that is either unnecessary, useless or foolish; find one line that you can improve, or that you can in any way equal; find a single sentence that does not fairly bristle all over with the divine heart and the infinite wisdom that prompted it:

"Let not your heart be troubled; ye believe in God, believe also in me.

"In my father's house are many mansions. I go to prepare a place for you.

"I am the true vine, and my father is the husbandman.

"Every branch in me that beareth not fruit he taketh away, and every branch that beareth fruit he purgeth it, that it may bring forth more fruit.

"Now ye are clean through the word which I have spoken unto you.

"Abide in me and I in you," etc., etc.

Could any merely human lips ever have given utterance to such words as these?

Let me read you one more selection from the Book of Mormon, page 305, Alma 16, 28:

"Therefore may God grant unto you, my brethren, that ye may begin to call upon his holy name, that he would have mercy upon you; yea, cry unto him for mercy for he is mighty to save; yea, humble yourselves and continue in prayer unto him; cry unto him when ye are in your fields; yea, over all your flocks: cry unto him in your houses, yea over all your household, both morning, mid-day and evening; yea, cry unto him against the power of your enemies; yea, cry unto him against the devil, who is an enemy to all righteousness. Cry unto him over the crops of your fields, that ye may prosper in them; cry over the flocks of your fields that they may increase. But this is not all; ye must pour out your souls in your closets and your secret places, and in your wilderness; yea, and when you do not cry unto the Lord, let your hearts be full, drawn out in prayer unto him continually for your welfare, and also for the welfare of those who are around you."

Friends, I have purposely read you one of the very best specimens to be found anywhere in the Book of Mormon, and have selected it because I wish frankly and freely to acknowledge that in many of the addresses and the exhortations scattered through the Book of Mormon, you may find good, sound, practical truths expressed, truths that will do you good and make your life better, if you can forgive the awkward, bungling manner in which they are usually expressed. And yet, if you closely scan any one of these earnest and practical addresses, you will find that nearly all that is valuable, or practicable, or beautiful in them *is borrowed from the Bible.* If you should strip them of all Biblical phraseology or Biblical thoughts, the refuse that is left would appear exceedingly human, never rising higher than the capacity of an ordinary man; a very ordinary man. There is not a passage in the book thus stripped of borrowed divinity that can at all equal in beauty, and power, and crispness, and elegance, the sentences or the thoughts of a multitude of human writers of the present day. How almost infinitely, then, do they fall below the character and the style of the sacred writers. Dear friends, to suppose that the great God would take the trouble to send an angel down from heaven to help any man of ordinary sense compose such sentences as these would be a repetition of the old fable, a mountain laboring to bring forth a mouse! And if the angel did come to help, and accomplish no more than this, he should forever hide his face in shame.

Perhaps you can see this point more clearly, if I read you a few specimens from what purports to be Jesus' own words. The book tells us, you remember, that Jesus, a few days after his ascension, as recorded in the New Testament, appeared here in this country and spent some forty days with his people, performing miracles and preaching to them the gospel of the kingdom. A goodly portion of his addresses are made up of the sermons on the mount, and various other selections from the four Gospels. But he throws in a great many other words. And friends, permit me to show you how vast the chasm between what he said here in this country and what he said in the Land of Judea, as to its style, its general character, especially in the one point, its terseness and comprehensiveness—the ability to "strike twelve" every time he utters a word.

'And while I read these specimens, please don't forget that the words repeated from his Judean life are in every instance quoted verbatim from our present English version, the King James' translation, which is supposed to be quite faulty; whereas the words he uttered here in this country are translated by the help of an angel, and therefore, of course, come to us pure from the ancient fountain.

The first selection is a single sentence, a rather long one, and somewhat mixed in its construction, but nevertheless is recorded as an actual speech from the lips of him who spake as never man spake, page 477, Nephi 9, 11:

"And behold, this is the thing which I will give unto you for a sign, for verily I say unto you, that when these things which I declare unto you and which I shall declare unto you hereafter of myself, and by the power of the Holy Ghost, which shall be given unto you of the Father, shall be made known unto the Gentiles, that they may know concerning this people, who are a remnant of the house of Jacob, and concerning this my people, who shall be scattered by them; verily, verily I say unto you, when these things shall be made known unto them of the Father, and shall come forth of the Father, from them unto you, for it is wisdom in the Father that they should be established in this land, and be set up as a free people by the power of the Father, that these things might come forth from them unto a remnant of your seed, that the covenant of the Father may be fulfilled which he has covenanted with his people, O house of Israel; therefore, when these works, and the works which shall be wrought among you hereafter, shall come forth from the Gentiles unto your seed, which shall dwindle in unbelief because of iniquity; for thus it behoveth the Father that it should come forth from the Gentiles, that he may show forth his power unto the Gentiles, for this cause, that the Gentiles, if they will not harden their hearts, that they may repent and come unto me, and be baptized in my name, and know of the true points of my doctrine, that they may be numbered among my people, O house of Israel; and when these things come to pass, that thy seed shall begin to know these things, it shall be a sign unto them, that they may know that the work of the Father hath already commenced, unto the fulfilling of the covenant which he hath made unto the people who are of the house of Israel."

This sentence contains over 340 words. The words "that" and "which" are repeated twenty times; the words "I," "my" and "me," eleven times; the word Father, eight times; Gentiles, five times; the expression, "shall come forth," four times. All this in one sentence. A very remarkable sentence surely.

I find upon examination that in Christ's sermon on the mount, beginning at the first sentence, 340 words include *eighteen complete sentences*, an average of *nineteen words to the sentence.* All Jesus' sentences found in the New Testament are short and incisive. The longest one I have been able to find is this one:

"Ye have heard that it hath been said, thou shalt love thy neighbor, and hate thine enemy: but I say unto you, love your enemies, bless them that curse you, do good to them that hate you, and pray for them which despitefully use you and persecute you; that ye may be the children of your Father which is in heaven: for he maketh his sun to rise on the evil and on the good; and sendeth rain on the just and on the unjust."

A very comprehensive, clear-cut sentence. No bungling, mixed up affair. How differently it sounds from the above bewildering mass of 340 words. Friends, can you believe Jesus was really the author of that long sentence? Does it sound like him? Can you find anything in the entire four Gospels that looks like it, that bears any resemblance whatever to it? Is it, as a sentence, the "forty-secondth cousin" of anything found in the four Gospels?

The second selection is from page 482, Nephi 11, 1:

"And it came to pass that when Jesus had expounded all the scriptures in one which they had written, he commanded them that they should teach the things which he had expounded unto them. And it came to pass that he commanded them that they should write the words which the Father had given unto Malachi, which he should tell unto them. And it came to pass that after they were written, he expounded them. And these are the words which he did tell unto them, saying, thus said the Father unto Malachi,"——

Now, mark you, what a wondrous transition from the above blundering, awkward narrative, to the majestic, sublime, and yet smooth and beautiful sentences that follow, quoted from the Bible:

"Behold I will send my messenger, and he shall prepare the way before me, and the Lord whom ye seek shall suddenly come to his temple, even the messenger of the covenant, whom ye delight in; behold, he shall come, saith the Lord of Hosts. But who may abide the day of his coming? and who shall stand when he appeareth? for he is like a refiner's fire and like fuller's soap. And he shall sit as a refiner and purifier of silver: and he shall purify the sons of Levi, and purge them as gold and silver, that they may offer unto the Lord an offering in righteousness."

Once more, please turn to page 485, Nephi 12, 3:

"And Jesus again showed himself unto them, for they were praying unto the Father, in his name; and Jesus came and stood in the midst of them, and saith unto them, what will ye that I shall give unto you? And they said unto him, Lord, we will that thou wouldst tell us the name whereby we shall call this church; for there are disputations among the people concerning this matter. And the Lord said unto them, verily, verily, I say unto you, why is it the people should murmur and dispute because of this thing? have they not read the scriptures, which say ye must take upon you the name of Christ, which is my name?* for by this name shall

---

*It is evident the Jesus who said this was a very ignorant man, and not the Jesus of the Gospels. "And she shall bring forth a son and they shall *call his name Jesus;* for he shall save his people from their sins. And he called his name Jesus."—Mathew 1: 21, 25. "And when eight days were accomplished for the circumcising of the child, his name was called Jesus, which was so named of the angel before he was conceived in the womb."—Luke 2: 21. The word "Christ" was not his name at all. It designated his *office*, "the Annointed One," "Jesus the Christ;" "Jesus the Annointed One," was the proper designation. Throughout the four Gospels, he is uniformly called Jesus. Wherever the word Christ occurs it was preceded by the emphatic article *the* in the Greek language, as in Matt. 16, 16. By frequent use, however, the article was after a while omitted, so that in the Epistles we find the two words associated together, Jesus Christ. *The article, however, is always understood.* So that his name was not "Christ," nor yet "Jesus Christ." It was simply Jesus. Hence, the author of the above unintentional *fib* could neither have been the Lord Jesus himself, nor any one inspired by his spirit.

ye be called at the last day; and whoso taketh upon him my name, and endureth to the end, the same shall be saved at the last day; therefore whatsoever ye shall do, ye shall do it in my name; therefore ye shall call the church in my name; and ye shall call upon the Father in my name, that he will bless the church for my sake: and how be it my church, save it be called in my name? for if a church be called in Moses' name, then it be Moses' church: or if it be called in the name of a man, then it be the church of a man; but if it be called in my name, then it is my church, if it so be that they are built upon my Gospel. Verily I say unto you that ye are built upon my Gospel; therefore ye shall call whatsoever things ye do in my name; therefore if ye call upon the Father, for the church, if it be in my name, the Father will hear you; and if it so be that the church is built upon my gospel, then will the Father show forth his own works in it; but if it be not built upon my gospel, and is built upon the works of men, or upon the works of the devil, verily I say unto you, they have joy in their works for a season, and by and by the end cometh and they are hewn down and cast into the fire, from whence there is no return; for their works do follow them, for it is because of their works that they are hewn down; therefore remember the things that I have told you."

Is there one before me to-night who can believe that such blundering sentences and worse than blundering statements, such puerile, shallow stuff, came from the lips of the Son of God, the man who spake as never man spake?

Bear with me once more, while I present another contrast, and I will not even stop to point out to you the place in the following quotation where the transition occurs between Jesus' words, as quoted from Isaiah the prophet, and Jesus' words as they profess to have come from his own lips, while here in this country. I think you will have no difficulty in deciding where the change occurs from the grand, lofty, sublime thought of the prophet Isaiah, to the coarse, awkward, bungling, mixed up sentences that are charged to our divine Lord.

I read from pages 480-1, Nephi 10, 2:

"O thou afflicted, tossed with tempest, and not comforted! behold, I will lay thy stones with fair colors, and lay thy foundation with sapphires. And I will make thy windows of agates, and thy gates of carbuncles, and all thy borders of pleasant stones. And all thy children shall be taught of the Lord; and great shall be the peace of thy children. In righteousness shalt thou be established; thou shalt be far from oppression, for thou shalt not fear, and from terror, for it shall not come near thee. Behold, they shall surely gather together against thee, not by me; whosoever shall gather together against thee shall fall for thy sake. Behold, I have created the smith that bloweth the coals in the fire, and that bringeth forth an instrument for his work; and I have created the waster to destroy. No weapon that is formed against thee shall prosper; and every tongue that shall rise against thee in judgment thou shalt condemn. This is the heritage of the servants of the Lord, and their righteousness is of me, saith the Lord. And now behold I say unto you, that ye had ought to search these things diligently; for great are the words of Isaiah. For surely he spake as touching all things concerning my people which are of the house of Israel; therefore it must needs be that he must speak also unto the Gentiles. And all things that he spake hath been and shall be, even according to the words which he spake. Therefore give heed to my words, write the things which I have told you; and according to the time and the will of the Father, they shall go forth unto the Gentiles."

And now, at this stage in the discussion, permit me to read you a passage where the poor man Nephi is made to give himself entirely away, so far as being inspired by the Holy Spirit or helped by an angel of God to write the book of Nephi. He *forgets* a very important matter of record; *leaves out* of his book an important fact that should have gone in it.—Page 481, Nephi 10, 3:

"And now it came to pass that when Jesus had said these words, he said unto them again, after he had expounded all the scriptures unto them which they had received, he said unto them, behold, other scriptures I would that ye should write, that ye have not. And it came to pass that he said unto Nephi, bring forth the record which ye have kept. And when Nephi had brought forth the records, and laid them before him, he cast his eyes upon them and said, verily I say unto you, I commanded my servant Samuel, the Lamanite, that he should testify unto this people, that at the day the Father should glorify his name in me, that there were many saints who should arise from the dead, and should appear unto many, and should minister unto them. And he said unto them, were it not so? And his disciples answered him and said, yea, Lord, Samuel did prophesy according to thy words, and they were all fulfilled. And Jesus said unto them, how be it that ye have not written this thing, that many saints did arise and appear unto many, and did minister unto them? And it came to pass that Nephi remembered that this thing had not been written And it came to pass that Jesus commanded that it should be written; therefore it was written as he commanded."

You readily see how it is. Jesus, in glancing over Nephi's record, discovers an important omission, *and chides Nephi for his neglect*. Nephi acknowledges the omission; and now, at the command of Jesus, inserts the omitted matter in at this place, entirely out of its proper connection. Now, was Nephi under the inspiration of the Holy Spirit or assisted by an angel from heaven when he made such a blunder as this in keeping his record? Is a patched up record inspired of God? If an angel comes all the way from heaven to help, it should have been an intelligent angel, blessed with a good memory, or he could have been of no particular advantage to Nephi.

But there are other proofs that this book must be a human production, that God could have had no hand whatever in its preparation, aside from the style in which it is written, and the blunder in the record just considered.

I ask your indulgence a few moments more, while I mention one other point. There are throughout the Book of Mormon numberless exhibitions of human weakness, altogether inconsistent with the supposition that it came from God.

For instance, each author is in the main the *hero of his own story*. Permit me to read you the opening sentence in the book, and simply call your attention to the fact that the words "I" and "my" occur *sixteen* times in this opening statement:

"I, Nephi, having been born of goodly parents, therefore I was taught somewhat in all the learning of my father; and having seen many afflictions in the course of my days, nevertheless, having been highly favored of the Lord in all my days; yea, having had a great knowledge of the goodness and mysteries of God, therefore, I make a record of my proceedings in my days; yea, I make a record in the language of my father, which consists of the learning of the Jews and the language of the Egyptians. And I know that the record which I make is true; and I make it with mine own hand; and I make it according to my knowledge."

For a specimen of real simon-pure conceit, read on next page, section 7:

"And now I, Nephi, do not make a full account of the things which my father hath written, for he hath written many things which he saw in visions and in dreams; and he also hath written many things which he prophesied and spake unto his children of which I shall not make a full account, but I shall make an account of my proceedings in my days. Behold, I make an abridgment of the record of my father, upon plates which I have made with my own hands; wherefore, after I have abridged the record of my father, then will I make an account of mine own life."

The second author, Jacob, begins his book thus, p. 114:

* * * "And he (Nephi) gave me, Jacob, a commandment that I should write upon these plates a few things which I considered to be most precious: that I should not touch, save it were lightly, concerning the history of this people which are called the people of Nephi. For he said that the history of his people should be engraven upon his other plates and that I should preserve these plates and hand them down unto my seed, from generation to generation. And if there were preaching which was sacred, or revelation which was great, or prophesying, that I should engraven the heads of them upon these plates, and touch upon them as much as it were possible. * * * And we also had many revelations, and the spirit of much prophesy."

The third author, Enos, begins his book by complimenting his father, Jacob,—a back-handed way of boasting over his own inherited good qualities, and the excellent training he had received—and then occupies a considerable space with an account of his own conversion, written in first-class modern revival style. While the fourth author, Jarom, modestly hints that the things he proposes to write are as nothing, compared with the things he had publicly taught and that had been revealed to him. And, in fact, this appears to be characteristic of nearly every author in the Book of Mormon, the modest boast, though, every little while repeated:

"I only record a very few of the remarkable revelations I have received, or of the remarkable deeds that have been accomplished through my leadership and inspiration."

Strikingly in contrast, this, with the authors of the various books of the Bible. The first book, Genesis, begins thus:

"In the beginning God created the heavens and the earth."

And we look at the close of the book, examine every page of it, in vain, to find even a hint as to who was its author. So with Exodus and Leviticus and Numbers; in fact, we have to read through over one half the entire Old Testament, embracing fifteen books, before we have so much as a hint of the authorship. The book of Nehemiah opens with this brief and modest title:

"The words of Nehemiah the son of Hachaliah."

Then, we pass the books of Esther, Job and the Psalms without the names of the authors. The Book of Proverbs has this preface:

"The Proverbs of Solomon, the son of David, King of Israel."

The various prophets are under a necessity, from the very character of their work, of revealing their names. But, it is done in the same, modest, simple way:

"The vision of Isaiah, the son of Amos, which he saw concerning Judah and Jerusalem."

"The words of Jeremiah, the son of Hilkiah, of the priests that were in Anathoth."

"The words of the Lord that came unto Hosea."

"The word of the Lord that came to Joel, the son of Pethuel."

"The words of Amos, who was among the herdmen of Tekoa."

And so with every one of the prophets. The opening sentence tells who is its author, but always in the *third* person, with the single exception of Ezekiel, who begins his prophesy in the *first* person.

If we examine the New Testament, we find Matthew begins thus:

"The book of the generations of Jesus Christ, the son of David, the son of Abraham."

Mark, thus:

"The beginning of the gospel of Jesus Christ, the son of God."

John, thus:

"In the beginning was the word, and the word was with God, and the word was God."

Luke is the only one of the four Evangelists who furnishes us anything like a *personal* introduction. And yet he entirely witholds his own name. The same with the Book of Acts. In fact we only learn from the early history of the church, entirely outside of the New Testament writers, *who wrote either one of these five books.*

With the Epistles it is, of course, different. They were private and personal affairs, addressed to individuals, as Timothy, Titus, &c., or they were addressed to particular churches and required the signature of the writer to give them value and authority at the time they were written. And yet one of the most important of the Epistles, the Book of Hebrews, remains incognito to this day, the best scholarship of the world being divided as to its real author. And not one of the authors becomes the hero of his own story, until we come to the prophets, who, in the most delicate way, with a modesty that has not the remotest suspicion of egotism, speak of themselves only when the necessities of the narrative requires such mention, as in the case of Isaiah, Jeremiah, Ezekiel and Daniel. Only one solitary author in the entire Bible makes a boast, or even mentions in any way whatever, the abundance of his revelations. And that is the Apostle Paul. And he was obliged to do it in vindication of the gospel he had preached, but apologizes in the most earnest and emphatic way for the necessity of thus *making a fool of himself*, as he calls it. "I am become a fool in glorying," he says to the Corinthians; "*ye have compelled me.*"

And do you know, friends, this is the way God has always wrought in nature? This world of ours is a wonderful world, crowded full of God's handiwork. Every grain of sand in it, every drop of water, every blade of grass, every shrub and flower, as well as every living thing that swims in its waters, or creeps upon its surface, or flies in its air, is full of proof—"the hand that made me is divine."

But now, friends, would not it seem a little strange, and somewhat out of keeping with the dignity and glory of the divine character, if God should attach a *label* to each separate article in nature, saying, "I made this."

If over each one of these beautiful shade trees were written, "This is my work," or suspended over every garden spot, or bed of flowers, or grassy meadow, in golden letters, "I, the Lord, did this;" or, if he should come down from heaven every evening in a cloud, and proclaim in thunder tones, that every one might hear, "All the blessings you have enjoyed to-day came from my hand." Surely this is not needful, friends, so long as the proofs of his handiwork lie all about us in such rich abundance.

Nor is it necessary for him to attach to the book of Genesis, or the book of Matthew, or John, or Hebrews, any affidavit whatever as to their inspired origin. Every page proclaims, "The brain that dictated this was an inspired brain." The necessity therefor that requires the various authors of the Book of Mormon to assert so frequently their divine inspiration, and parade upon almost every second or third page the abundance of their revelations, is a confession of weakness, to say the least, and suggests the suspicion that the author fears you may not find out the divine origin of his plates unless he keeps reiterating the fact—the sad necessity of the young painter, you remember, whose first attempt at painting proved so far a failure that he was obliged to write underneath his picture, "*This is a horse!*"

The next lecture will show that the Book of Mormon is wholly a *modern* composition, and therefore not at all what it professes to be.

LECTURE III.

"For my thoughts are not your thoughts, neither are your ways my ways, saith the Lord.

"For as the heavens are higher than the earth, so are my ways higher than your ways, and my thoughts than your thoughts."—Isaiah 55, 8-9.

The other day, a neighbor of mine was examining somewhat minutely a few of the *worms*, or caterpillars with which out city is infested. Calling my attention to them, I discovered for the first time, that they were not the muddy, dirty-looking, ugly creatures I had supposed. A close inspection revealed the fact that they were really beautiful; that an exquisite taste had been displayed in the various colors employed, their skillful blending, and the delicateness and perfection of their tints, and especially in the strange and endless variety exhibited. Really, you could find no two exactly alike.

And then there suddenly flashed upon me a fact I was taught when a school-boy, that there are no two objects in nature exactly alike; infinite *variety* and not *sameness* is the rule. And I recall hours spent with brothers and sisters in the old home garden, examining a large bed of "ribbon grass" to test the theory. There were only a few colored lines on each blade of grass, but they were always arranged differently, so that we never found two exactly alike. Extending our observation, we patiently examined hundreds and thousands of clover leaves, the leaves upon the apple trees, and the leaves upon the small oak saplings, growing in a neighboring pasture, and always with the same result; no two alike.

We all know that there are no two human faces just alike, no two human characters alike. All possess the same contour of face, the same faculties, passions and attributes; but the varieties of development are apparently infinite, so that, probably, no two persons have ever lived, or ever will live, who look and act and are exactly alike. And it is said that the same law of infinite variety extends even to the minutest animacule that appears in a drop of water, and lives but a brief day; to every grain of sand upon the sea shore; in fact, as some believe, to every ultimate, minute particle of matter of which our earth is composed.

And, friends, this endless variety, exhibited everywhere in nature, affording us such clear proof of the limitless, the unbounded resources of the great Creator, is found just as clearly marked in the Bible. There are certain great lines of truth distinctly and clearly revealed to us; but the unfolding of these great lines of truth is almost infinitely varied. So that there are, properlyspeaking, *no repetitions* in the Bible. There are repetitions of questions and commands for the sake of added emphasis; sometimes of words and phrases required by the bold and vigorous and animated style of the Holy Scriptures; yet, properly speaking, the Bible does not repeat itself. The New Testament does not repeat the Old Testament; none of the later books repeat from the earlier books. There is one single instance in the Old Testament where one short chapter is repeated word for word in two different books. Why, we do not know. Probably, two different authors, in making a record or compiling a history of the same personages, had access to the same original document and quoted them alike. In the New Testament, three different men, Matthew, Mark and Luke, furnish a history of the life of Christ. They write entirely independent of each other, in separate portions of the world, for entirely different classes of people, and evidently without any knowledge of each others work; and, as might be expected, when recording the same event, mention the very same particulars, the prominent points in the event they narrate. But, they scarcely ever *do it in the same words*. Each presents the fact from his own standpoint; and, hence, exhibits a different phase from the other, keeping up a constant freshness and variety. Even in the large number of quotations found in the New Testament from the Old, the language is so varied as to present a new side to the old truth, giving you a view of it that you had not been able to discover from the Old Testament reading. And, the quotations from the Old Testament found in the New are exceedingly brief; the longest one is in Rom. 3, quoted from the Psalms, to prove that "there is none righteous." And this quotation embraces only three brief sentences, making in all eight or ten lines on a printed page like this.

If it had been different, if one prophet had quoted large portions of a previous prophet's words, if the New Testament writers had borrowed whole chapters from the Old Testament prophets and made up their addresses chiefly in this way, we would at once have felt, "Something is out of joint: the God of nature and the God of the Bible seem to proceed differently. And, has God really exhausted his resources in the Old Testament revelations, that he must needs repeat himself thus? Has he *nothing new* to tell us? not even a *new way* of presenting the old thoughts?"

Well, now, friends, the Book of Mormon has this very serious objection to its divinity: *It is not original enough to have come from God.* It is made up largely of *borrowed* material. Outside of the mere frame work of the book, its thread of history, the filling in is largely borrowed. I mean the religious part of the book; its sermons, exhortations and addresses are either repetitions of the exact language of the Bible, or they are constructed as gospel sermons of the present day-are constructed, filled in with a large amount of Bible phraseology, Bible allusions, illustrations, etc.

For instance, I find that the Lord Jesus, when he first appeared to the Nephites, as recorded in the fifth chapter of III Nephi, after saying a few words (more than one half of which are selections* from his various words as recorded in the four Gospels), began to repeat the Sermon on the Mount, as recorded by Matthew in the 5th, 6th and 7th chapters, and repeated the entire sermon word for word. Then followed this, with about as much more material filled in constantly with short phrases or whole sentences taken from other portions of the Bible. When he came back the second time and addressed them at some length, he quotes verbatim nearly two whole chapters from the book of Isaiah, and closes up his speech with a repetition of the two last chapters of the Book of Malachi.

---

*The following is a specimen. The *borrowed* words and phrases are in italics. (See III Nephi, 5, 9.): "And *again I say unto you*, ye must *repent, and be baptized* in my name, and *become as a little child*, or *ye can in nowise inherit the kingdom of God. Verily, verily I say unto you*, that this is my doctrine, and *whoso buildeth upon this, buildeth upon* my *rock, and the gates of hell shall not prevail against* them. And whoso shall declare more or less than this, and establish it for my doctrine, *the same cometh of evil*, and is not *built upon* my *rock*, but he *buildeth upon a sandy foundation*, and the *gates of hell* standeth open to receive such, when the *floods come and the winds beat upon them*.

I find in the second book of Nephi, beginning with the eighth chapter, the author quotes from Isaiah, the prophet, and fills up *sixteen full pages*, transcribing the greater part of the first fourteen chapters of Isaiah's prophecy. Nearly the whole of Isaiah, and occasional selections from the other prophets, are thus incorporated into the Book of Mormon, with the major portion of Christ's words as found in the four evangelists, and a generous sprinkling from all the epistles and the Book of Revelation.

It is no excuse for this lack of originality and constant repetition of the Bible, that, while it was not new to us, *it was new to the people in this country who heard it*. There could have been no possible objection to having those old sermons and addresses filled up with Bible quotations for the benefit of those who listened to them; but, such quotations should have been left out of a record that was kept for us who already possess the Bible. And, that ancient record, as is frequently asserted, *was made for us exclusively*, and not for the people then living. They had nothing whatever to do with the plates from which the Book of Mormon was translated; in fact, *never saw them*.* They were prepared and preserved for our bene-

---

* It is understood that the entire Book of Mormon, except the last *fifty Pages*, was written by one Mormon, who lived just at the close of the Nephite history; was commander-in-chief of the Nephite forces in that terrible battle that swept the Nephite nation out of existence in the year 384 after Christ. The plates of the elder Nephi, his brother Jacob, and all their successors in office for nearly a thousand years, came into the hands of Mormon, and he *made an abridgement in his own language,* and then turned this abridgement over to the safe keeping of his son Moroni, who completes the record and hides it in the hill Cumorah to be found by Joseph Smith in our day. Mormon's plain statement is (See pages 141-2, "Words of Mormon," sec. 2-3-4.): "For after I had *made an abridgement* from the plates of Nephi down to the reign of this king Benjamin * * * And now I, Mormon, proceed to finish out my record, which I take from the plates of Nephi; and I make it according to the knowledge and the understanding which God has given me * * * and I cannot write the hundredth part of the things of my people."

The plates, then, found by Joseph Smith, and from which this Book of Mormon was translated, are not the *original records* kept by the various kings and prophets, but an abridgement, and a very brief one, made by Mormon; and were never seen, except by the son Moroni, until they came into Joseph Smith's hands.

fit alone. And it is altogether a work of supererogation to furnish us the same message twice over. Jesus said a thousand things that are not left on record for us, and so did Paul and the other apostles, and undoubtedly, in their preaching, often quoted largely from the Old Testament, very likely whole chapters at a time. But such sermons and such quotations were not left on record for us, because we have all such passages already in the Old Testament, and God *never does unnecessary things.*

We must, therefore, conclude that at least so much of these plates as contain such large repetitions of the Old and New Testaments cannot have been recorded at the command of God for our benefit, unless he would do in this country what he never would do in the old.

But aside from these direct quotations from the Bible, there are found many Bible passages with *variations in the way of attempted improvements, or embellishments.* Let me read you an illustration.—Page 454, Nephi 4: 10:

"And it came to pass that there came a voice again unto the people, and all the people did hear, and did witness of it, saying, O ye people of these great cities which have fallen, who are descendants of Jacob, yea, who are of the house of Israel, how oft have I gathered you as a hen gathers her chickens under her wings, and have nourished you. And again, how oft would I have gathered you as a hen gathereth her chickens under her wings; yea, O ye people of the house of Israel, who have fallen; yea, O ye people of the house of Israel, ye that dwell at Jerusalem, as ye that have fallen; yea, how oft would I have gathered you as a hen gathereth her chickens, and ye would not. O ye house of Israel whom I have spared, how oft will I gather you as a hen gathereth her chickens under her wings if ye will repent and turn unto me with full purpose of heart. But if not, O house of Israel, the places of your dwelling shall become desolate until the time of the fulfilling of the covenant to your fathers."

One of the most beautiful incidents recorded in the New Testament, Christ blessing little children, (see Matthew, 19, 13-15,) occupying three short verses, is in this way embellished and improved upon until it has the appearance of an exhibition gotten up for a show; is unnatural and distorted, and thoroughly at variance with the beautiful simplicity of our Savior's character.—Page 468, Nephi, 8: 4, 5:

"And it came to pass that he commanded that their little children should be brought. So they brought their little children and set them down upon the ground round about him, and Jesus stood in the midst; and the multitude gave way till they all had been brought unto him. And it came to pass that when they had all been brought, and Jesus stood in the midst, he commanded the multitude that they should kneel down upon the ground. And it came to pass that when they had knelt upon the ground, Jesus groaned within himself, and saith, Father, I am troubled because of the wickedness of the people of the house of Israel. And when he had said these words, he himself also knelt upon the earth; and behold he prayed unto the Father, and the things which he prayed cannot be written, and the multitude did bear record who heard him. And after this manner do they bear record: the eye hath never seen, neither hath the ear heard, before, so great and marvelous things as we saw and heard Jesus speak unto the Father; and no tongue can speak, neither can there be written by any man, neither can the hearts of men conceive so great and marvelous things as we both saw and heard Jesus speak; and no one can conceive of the joy which filled our souls at the time we heard him pray for us unto the Father.

"And it came to pass that when Jesus had made an end of praying unto the Father, he arose; but so great was the joy of the multitude that they were overcome. And it came to pass that Jesus spake unto them and bade them arise. And they arose from the earth, and he said unto them, blessed are ye because of your faith. And now behold my joy is full. And when he had said these words, he wept, and the multitude bear record of it, and he took their little children, one by one, and blessed them, and prayed unto the Father for them. And when he had done this he wept again, and he spake unto the multitude, and saith unto them, behold your little ones. And as they looked to behold, they cast their eyes toward heaven, and they saw the heavens open, and they saw angels descending out of heaven as it were, in the midst of fire, and they came down and encircled those little ones about, and they were encircled about with fire; and the angels did minister unto them, and the multitude did see and hear and bear record; and they knew that their record is true; for they all of them did see and hear every man for himself; and they were in number about two thousand and five hundred souls; and they did consist of men, women and children."

Just previous to this, in the presence of the same congregation of 2500, we have another little New Testament incident embellished and improved upon until it amounts to little less than a travesty or burlesque. In Jno. 20: 27, the doubting Thomas is permitted to feel the print of the nails in the risen Savior's hands, and to thrust his hand into the sword wound in the side, to strengthen his wavering faith in his risen Lord. But now, read page 456, Nephi 5: 6, 7:

"And it came to pass that the Lord spake unto them, saying, arise and come forth unto me, that ye may thrust your hands into my side, and also that ye may feel the prints of the nails in my hands and in my feet, that ye may know that I am the God of Israel, and the God of the whole earth, and have been slain for the sins of the world.

"And it came to pass that the multitude went forth and thrust their hands into his side, and did feel the prints of the nails in his hands and in his feet; and this they did do, going forth, one by one, until they had all gone forth, and did see with their eyes, and did feel with their hands, and did know of a surety, and did bear record, that it was he of whom it was written by the prophets that should come."

Just think of it, friends, 2500 people go forth one by one and "thrust their hands into his side, and did feel the print of the nails in his hands and in his feet." It would be very rapid work, requiring so much haste as to give the whole thing the appearance of a farce, to suppose *five* persons could thus pass the Savior every minute, giving each one only *twelve seconds* to thrust his hand into the side and feel the print of the nails both in his hands and in his feet. But at this rapid rate it would require just *eight hours and twenty minutes of time!*

The author of the Book of Mormon must have had a *wonderful development of the marvelous* in his make up, for a large number of the incidents and the miracles of the Bible are in this way improved upon, until the impression siezes hold upon you that the author is bent upon *beating the Bible*, casting its miracles and its wonderful incidents completely in the shade, at whatever strain upon the readers credulity, or sacrifice of reason or common sense.

For instance, the three hours of darkness extending over the land of Judea, and the earthquake and the rending of the rocks, that accompanied the Savior's agony upon the cross, as if nature were expressing sympathy with her suffering Creator, and that ceased when his agonized soul was released, is not only repeated here in this country, but is extended through three full days; with such a darkness as remands that old miracle in Egypt to the shades; and with such accompaniments as the eye never saw or pen ever recorded before or since. Its account occupies four and a half pages, being chapter four of Nephi, pages 450-455.*

The birth of Jesus Christ was signalized in his own homeland by two beautiful and appropriate occurrences: the appearance of a star to guide the eastern magi to his birthplace, and the angels appearance and announcement to the watchful shepherds on the plains of Bethlehem, neither of which was seen or heard by any other parties. But how little and insignificant compared with the occurrences on this continent that same night! The people had been prepared by years of prophesying and were on the tiptoe of expectancy as the designated time drew near. As the year was ushered in, "Behold the prophesies of the prophets began to be fulfilled more fully,

---

*For a full account of this remarkable occurrence, please see next lecture.

for there began to be greater signs and greater miracles wrought among the people." But there were wicked unbelievers in those days, and they were cruel enough to set apart a day "that all those who believed in these traditions shouldbe put to death, except the sign should come to pass which had been given by Samuel the prophet."

At this the good Nephi's heart became "exceeding sorrowful. And it came to pass that he went out and bowed himself down upon the earth and cried mightily unto the Lord all the day; and, behold the voice of the Lord came unto him, saying, lift up your head and be of good cheer, for, behold the time is at hand, and on this night shall the sign be given, and on the morrow come I into the world."

And sure enough this promise was fulfilled.

* * * "For behold at the going down of the sun there was no darkness; and the people began to be astonished, because there was no darkness when the night came. And there were many, who had not believed the words of the prophets, fell to the earth and became as if they were dead * * * yea, in fine, all the people upon the face of the whole earth, from the west to the east, both in the land north (North America) and in the land south (South America,) were so exceedingly astonished that they fell to the earth; for they knew that the prophets had testified of these things for many years, and that the sign which had been given was already at hand; and they began to fear because of their iniquity and their unbelief.

"And it came to pass that there was no darkness in all that night, but it was as light as though it was midday. And it came to pass that the sun did rise in the morning again, according to its proper order; and they knew that it was the day that the Lord should be born, because of the sign which had been given. And it came to pass also, that a new star did appear, according to the word."

Friends, this is evidently the most stupendous physical miracle ever accomplished since God first called the sun into being, for the sun goes down as usual and is seen to rise the next morning at its proper time; hence, the Creator, in some monster chemical laboratory, must manufacture light to furnish both these vast continents enough to make it "as light as though it was midday" for twelve consecutive hours; or else suspend some huge *reflector* at such an angle in mid-heavens as to throw upon these two continents the full power of the sun's rays during the whole night. Joshua's miracle of lengthening a day by commanding the sun to stand still was mere child's play compared with this! Evidently, no ordinary miracles can satisfy the versatile genius and the brilliant imagination of the author of this book.

One more illustration. The building of Noah's ark is completely cast into the shade by the feat of Jared and his company, who built *eight barges, or vessels*, all "according to the instructions of the Lord." Let me read you from Ether, 1: 5—page 519:

"And it came to pass that the brother of Jared did go to work, and also his brother, and built barges after the manner which they had built, according to the instructions of the Lord. And they were small, and they were light upon the water, even like unto the lightness of a fowl upon the water; and they were built after a manner that they were exceeding tight, even that they would hold water like unto a dish; and the bottom thereof was tight like unto a dish; and the sides thereof were tight like unto a dish; and the ends thereof were peaked; and the top thereof was tight like unto a dish; and the length thereof was the length of a tree; and the door thereof, when it was shut, was tight, like unto a dish."

When they are finished the brother of Jared "cried unto the Lord saying, O Lord, I have performed the work which thou hast commanded me, and I have made the barges according as thou hast directed me."

Please notice, friends, that they are built exactly "*according to the instructions of the Lord.*" But lo and behold! the Lord has *forgotten* two very important matters.

a. No *ventilation* has been provided—as tight as an egg-shell—and so the brother of Jared informs the Lord of the omission.

"And also we shall perish, for in them we cannot breathe, save it is the air which is in them; therefore we shall perish. And the Lord said unto the brother of Jared, behold, thou shalt make a hole in the top thereof, and also in the bottom thereof; and when thou shalt suffer for air, thou shalt unstop the hole thereof, and receive air. And if so be that the water come in upon thee, behold ye shall stop the hole thereof, that ye may not perish in the flood. And it came to pass that the brother of Jared did so, according as the Lord had commanded."

The exact object of the hole in the bottom does not clearly appear; nor is it stated how they are to get air to breathe when the waves are breaking over them so fiercely that they have to close the hole at the top; for the sequel tells us positively:

"And it came to pass that they were many times buried in the depths of the sea, because of the mountain waves which broke upon them, and also the great and terrible tempests which were caused by the fierceness of the wind."

b. But now another sad deficiency is discovered:

"And he cried again unto the Lord saying, O Lord, behold I have done even as thou hast commanded me; and I have prepared the vessels for my people, and behold there is no light in them. Behold, O Lord, wilt thou suffer that we shall cross the great water in darkness?"

And the Lord, apparently, is puzzled to know how to manage this matter, and so he asks advice of the brother of Jared:

"And the Lord said unto the brother of Jared, what will ye that I should do that ye may have light in your vessels? For behold, ye cannot have windows, for they will be dashed in pieces; neither shall ye take fire with you, for ye shall not go by the light of fire; for behold, ye shall be as a whale in the midst of the sea; for the mountain waves shall dash upon you. Nevertheless, I will bring you up again out of the depths of the sea; for the winds have gone forth out of my mouth, and also the rains and the floods have I sent forth. And behold, I prepare you against these things; for howbeit, ye cannot cross this great deep, save I prepare you against the waves of the sea, and the winds which have gone forth, and the floods which shall come. Therefore what will ye that I should prepare for you that ye may have light when ye are swallowed up in the depths of the sea?"

And the brother of Jared was quite equal to the emergency. He was evidently a man of remarkable resources. He went up into a very high mountain "and did moulten out of a rock sixteen small stones, and they were white and clear even as transparent glass."*

And those sixteen stones he presented before the Lord; and after an earnest prayer, in which he informs the Lord of his ability to do anything he pleases, he says:

"Therefore touch these stones, O Lord, with thy finger, and prepare them that they may shine forth in the darkness; and they shall shine forth unto us in the vessels which we have prepared, that we may have light while we shall cross the sea."

And the Lord did so, and touched the stones one by one with his finger, and they became luminous with light, and were placed two in each barge, one at each end.

"And it came to pass that when they had prepared all manner of food, that thereby they might subsist upon the water and also food for their flocks and herds, and whatsoever beast, or animal, or fowl that they should carry with them. And it came to pass that when they had done all these things, they got aboard of their vessels or barges, and set forth into the sea, commending themselves unto the Lord their God."

Perhaps we should not stop to cavil over such small matters as to *who* pushed these vessels, or barges, off the shore when they were all loaded; nor how they managed for 344 days without *fresh water* to drink; nor yet the statement, "And it came to pass that the Lord God caused that there should a *furious wind* blow upon the face of the waters *toward the promised land*," and that this wind continued to blow furiously in one direction, day

---

*Just a little *early* in the history of the race (100 years after the flood) to speak of glass.

and night, for 344 days, driving them through the Indian Ocean and across the mighty Pacific, through its gulf streams and all, meanwhile keeping all those eight barges together and landing them all safely on the shores of the new world! A miracle compared with which all the ordinary miracles of the Bible are tame and almost insipid.

There are several other historical incidents, founded upon Bible narratives, with attempted improvements, that I had hoped to review this evening, but time will allow only a reference, such as the building of a temple after the pattern of Solomon's temple, by six or eight men and a few boys, in the space of perhaps three or four years (the exact time not given, but it could not have been more), while Solomon's temple required seven years and the employment of 153,300 men.—See II Nephi, 4: 3. The beheading of John the Baptist, accomplished through the dancing of Herodias; worked over by the daughter of Jared, who sought to secure through her dancing the head of her grandfather. —See Ether, 3: 11, 12.

Joshua's plan of capturing Ai by an ambush, made to do valuable service against the enemies of the Nephites on at least two different occasions.—See Alma, 26: 22, 31. Numerous other Bible incidents, worked over until the plagiarism is almost hidden from view by the extra embellishments; all of which look very much unlike God, and partake very much of human weakness.

But, we are not yet done with these Bible quotations.

Suppose a man, to-day, should write a book and attach to it the name of some noted author of *two hundred* years ago, and attempt to make the world believe that it really was the production of that old author, hidden from the public, for certain reasons, until now. How could the truth be ascertained? In several ways; one way would be this:

During the past 200 years, our English language has been undergoing a great many changes; many old words have become obsolete and are no longer used, while thousands of new words have been coined from the various languages with which our language has come in contact, or have grown out of important events, or revolutions, or scientific discoveries that have during these 200 years occurred. Now, if upon examination, this book, purporting to be 200 years old, is found to be written in the current language of the present day, full of words and phrases and idiomatic expressions that were wholly unknown to the English language 200 years ago, this fact alone would furnish the most conclusive possible proof of the fraud. It could not have been written 200 years ago. It must have been written during the present age.

An actual illustration of this method of criticism, and the certainty of its results, may be of interest.

In all the old copies of our Bible, you will remember, there used to be found between the Old and the New Testaments, a number of books called the "*Apocraphy.*" The time was, in the early ages of the Christian church, when a large majority of the Christians in the world believed those books were inspired of God, and therefore should have a place in the Bible. Not time this evening to explain to you how this came about, though it is a very interesting page of history. I will simply select one of these books and show how easily careful students have ascertained, beyond the possibility of question, that it is *spurious*. I refer to the book called the "Book of Wisdom." It is a beautiful book, in many particulars, finely composed; is, in fact, one of the finest human compositions of ancient times. But it professes to have been written by *Solomon*, the great king Solomon, son of David. Now, Solomon lived 1000 years before Christ, at a time when the Hebrew language was written and spoken in its purity; and all Solomon's writings that have come down to us in the Old Testament scriptures are found in the Hebrew language.

Four hundred years after the death of Solomon, the Jewish nation was carried in captivity to Babylon, the capital of Chaldea. There they remained seventy years; and the pure Hebrew of the Jews came in constant contact with the Chaldaic language. The result was perfectly natural. The Jews learned to make use of a large number of Chaldaic words and phrases and idioms. The pure Hebrew became corrupted by having incorporated into it a large amount of the Chaldaic. This mixture is very clearly seen in the Book of Daniel, the books of Ezra and Nehemiah, the prophecies of Ezekiel and all the minor prophets who wrote during the time or after the captivity at Babylon. Their writings are full of *Chaldaisms* that is, words and phrases and peculiar idioms that they learned to use while living in Babylon.

Now, this "Book of Wisdom" just mentioned, is *filled full of Chaldaisms*, or Chaldaic words and phrases and idiomatic expressions which had not been heard of, or found in the Hebrew language *for at least four hundred years after the death of Solomon*. Proving beyond the possibility of a doubt that the book was written either during, or after the captivity at Babylon; and, of course, was not written by Solomon. And therefore a fraud—a lie upon the face of it—an attempt to deceive the public, and gain for itself credit and influence, and perhaps divine authority by forging the name of that wisest and most illustrious of men, Solomon, as its author.

In a similar way has been shown the spurious character of a multitude of books written in the first, second and third centuries after Christ, purporting to be authentic lives of Jesus Christ, or genuine letters of the apostles, with an apostle's name attached. They are either written in the current language of their day, and thus easily betray their real age, or else the attempt to imitate the apostles' style and language is too apparent to deceive the critical scholar. "Murder will out." In every attempt at fraud, the cloven foot will show itself somewhere, however careful and determined the effort to cover it up.

Well now, the Book of Mormon purports to have been written, the first part of it, by a Jew named Nephi, a son of Lehi, who left the city of Jerusalem with his father in the reign of Zedekiah, king of Judah, or about six hundred years before Christ. Nearly one fourth of the entire book was written by this man Nephi; the balance was written by his brother Jacob and their descendants, covering a period of nearly one thousand years.*
The entire book was written or engraven upon plates in a sort of Hebraized Egyptian language, or, as the author states it:

"I make a record in the language of my father, which consists of the learning of the Jews and the language of the Egyptians," whatever that may mean. I believe the last writer Moroni decides upon naming this nondescript language the "Reformed Egyptian." And

---
*Properly speaking, Mormon and his son Moroni wrote the entire book, but Nephi and his descentants, as above stated, *furnished all the material*;

I must frankly confess to you, friends, *I do not like the look of this. It has the scent of fraud in it.*

The pure Hebrew was, at the time Nephi left Jerusalem, the *native tongue* of the Jews; it was *exclusively their written language*. Every book in the Old Testament up to that time had been written in the pure Hebrew. And how this man, who, the book tells us, was born and raised right in the city of Jerusalem, could have used from his childhood the Egyptian language, is indeed singular, considering the Jews' *hatred* of the Egyptians, and their strong veneration amounting almost to adoration of their native Hebrew.

And the singularity of the thing is only increased when we remember that the Egyptian language was a very awkward, unwieldly, cumbersome and frequently unintelligible language as compared with the Hebrew, which was the most beautiful, expressive and comprehensive language then in use, peculiarly well adapted to be the medium for communicating God's thoughts and God's wisdom to the world. In fact, the prophet Moroni frankly admits this superiority of the Hebrew over the reformed Egyptian. He says:

"And now behold we have written this record according to our knowledge in the characters which are called among us, the reformed Egyptian, being handed down and altered by us according to our manner of speech. And if our plates had been sufficiently large, we should have written in Hebrew; but the Hebrew hath been altered by us also; and if we could have written in the Hebrew, behold ye would have had no imperfection in our record. But the Lord knoweth the things which we have written, and also that none other people knoweth our language."—Mormon, 4: 8.

This statement is positive, that had we used the Hebrew instead of the Reformed Egyptain there would have been "no imperfection* in our record."

---

*A lame and silly attempt, this, at finding an excuse for all the blunders and imperfections in style, etc., already pointed out in the Book of Mormon.

And now, friends, what do you imagine can be the reason, what vast and weighty consideration can be a sufficient inducement to allow blunders and imperfections enough to curse the book forever, and prove that it could never have been inspired of God? when by simply using the Hebrew language all would have been as perfect and complete as the most exacting could desire, "no imperfection in our record."

The reason given is, that his *plates were not large enough* for the Hebrew. "If our plates had been sufficiently large we should have written in Hebrew." That is, the Hebrew requires *more space* than the Egyptian. Friends, I can characterize this by no smoother language than that it is a *bold and impudent lie*, evidently designed to cover the real reason why the plates were found in the Reformed Egyptian.

a. To show you the difference between the Egyptian and the Hebrew languages, both as to the space they occupy, and the ease of writing, or engraving upon plates, I have had transcribed the following two words as specimens, taken from the Edinburgh Encyclopedia, article "Hieroglyphics" (Egyptian):

Hebrew.	Pronounced.	Meaning.
מֶרְכֶּבֶת	Mirkebeth.	Chariot.
Egyptian.		
[Egyptian glyphs]	Markabuta.	Chariot.
Hebrew.		
כִּנּוֹר	Kinnor.	Harp.
Egyptian.		
[Egyptian glyphs]	Kenaanauor.	Harp.

And that these two Egyptian words are by no means exceptional* ones can be very easily seen by anyone who will examine the very exhaustive article above mentioned.

b. But even if the statement from Moroni were true, if the Hebrew required larger plates, if it required *ten fold* more space than the Reformed Egyptian, the excuse would come with ill grace in a book that has more plates in it, and more said about them, than any book, perhaps, ever written. All the way from the first Nephi to Mormon, plates, almost by the wagon load, are mentioned. The following are only a few of the places where plates in great abundance are mentioned:

See pages 2, 3, 11, 16, 44, 62, 63, 138, 139, 141, 142, 144, 145, 161, 162, 204, 394, 395, 549.† In three places at least, Mormon says that his *abridgement* from all these various records contains less than one hundredth part of the originals that were in his hands.

"But behold, a hundredth part of the proceedings of this people cannot be contained in this work; but behold, there are many books and many records of every kind, and they have been kept chiefly by the Nephites; and they have been handed down from one generation to another by the Nephites."—Heleman, 2: 4, or p. 394. See also pages 142 and 549.

All these writings, remember, claim to be inspired of God, and were engraven at his command, *one hundred times more than were needed for this Book of Mormon.* One may, therefore, be excused for calling into question the statement that there were not plates enough

---

*Among the pure hieroglyphics an occasional word occurs exceedingly brief. Instance the happy conception that made a simple *circle* represent the word *eternity*. But these brief word signs were the exception; when words were *spelled out* in the usual way, they occupy two or three times as much space as the Hebrew. See also foot note on page 74.

†The edition of the Book of Mormon I use was published in Salt Lake, in 1876, by David O. Calder.

to allow the use of the Hebrew, and thus have secured "no imperfection in our record," when a hundred times more material than was actually needed had already been engraven upon plates, at the command of God.

Why then, friends, should Nephi and his successors to the time of Moroni, have rejected their own native language, so well adapted to the work they had in hand, and have selected, instead, a language they freely acknowledge is imperfect, and poorly fitted for their use, and then attempt to deceive their readers as to the *real reason, unless the supposition of fraud is the true explanation.*

Mr. Smith and his helpers, if he had such, were certainly sharp enough to know that had they represented those plates to have been written in the Hebrew language, there were a thousand Hebrew scholars all over the world, who could easily and readily have exposed the fraud. For the words and phrases and idioms of that language are so peculiar; its way of expressing thought so different from any other language on earth that no honest or correct translation could possibly hide or cover up its peculiarities. But by having those plates engraved in a language that no person at the present day knew anything about, *no scholar on earth could detect the fraud in the usual way.* The criticisms would be placed outside the pale of oriental scholarship at least.

And yet, friends, there are some rules, some facts, that must be true even of the Egyptian language after it has been mixed up with "the learning of the Jews." And one fact is that the Egyptian language had *only a few words in it.* The Hebrew, as compared with the other ancient languages, is universally acknowledged to be exceedingly rich and comprehensive. And yet the total number of words in it is limited to a few thousand; and its primary words, its roots, the foundations of the language, are limited to a few hundred. And the same thing was necessarily true of all the earliest languages on the earth.* Language is a growth. As different nations, and diverse peoples mingle with each other, rub against each other, new ideas are formed, new facts discovered, new thoughts developed; and, therefore, *new words have to be coined* to express those new thoughts. Hence, the Greek and the Latin languages, being a later growth than either the Hebrew or the Egyptian, are found with a greatly *enlarged vocabulary*. The Latin, for instance, has several times as many words in it as the older Hebrew.

And even more rapid has been the change in modern times, keeping pace with the rapid strides in every branch of human learning, until our *English* language is fairly loaded down with the wealth of all the past; and contains, probably, *twenty times* as many words as either the ancient Hebrew or the Egyptian. And thousands of these words are, of course, *new words*, made necessary to express new thoughts, new facts in science, new facts in human experience, new views of truth, enlarged conceptions of old truths that require new forms of ex-

---

*The first attempt of the Egyptians, in the earliest age, to reduce their spoken language to writing, was the invention of what are called *"hieroglyphics,"* a system of symbol, or sign writing; for instance, they wished to write the word "horse;" having no alphabet, or letters of any kind, no way of *spelling* the word, they made a *picture* of a horse; a stairway was represented by a few steps; a tree, bird, etc., by the thing itself in outline. Thus every object in nature was expressed so far as possible by its picture, while *ideas* not objects, were expressed by certain symbols; as, the word eternity, by a circle; weakness, by a human form bending over etc., etc. When this method of writing had reached its limit, the language was found to contain about 900 words, altogether.

Intercourse with other nations, probably, after a time suggested the invention of an alphabet with letters representing the elementary sounds of their spoken language, with what success, the two specimens on page 71 will show.

pression. There are thousands of words, therefore, that express thoughts and facts and ideas that were never dreamed of in the earlier ages of the world; and that no word or combination of words in the ancient Hebrew or Egyptian could express.

If, therefore, upon a careful examination of the Book of Mormon, any such words shall be found in it, words or phrases or forms of expression conveying thoughts that are known to be entirely modern, wholly unknown to either the Hebrew or the Egyptian language anciently, this would furnish the most indubitable proof that the book is a *modern composition*, and therefore not what it claims to be.

Time will allow the mention of only a few words by way of illustration.

And the first word that attracted my attention at the very beginning of the book, was the name of Lehi's *third son, Sam.* I said to myself, "Sam, Sam, Sam. Well, really, here is a boy six hundred years before Christ who has the bonifide Yankee nickname for Samuel." There is certainly nothing *Hebrewistic* about this name, nor does it sound like any Egyptian name we ever heard; possibly, however, by putting the Hebrew and the Egyptian languages together, or by adding to the Egyptian "the learning of the Jews," this name, "Sam," might be manufactured. I would not, therefore, offer this as *conclusive* evidence of the modern origin of the book, but I confess it started in my own mind the first grave *suspicion* in that direction.

But here is a word, on page 206, that by no possible chance could have been used in those early ages:

"I myself have laboured with all the power of faculties which I have possessed."

"Faculty" is from the Latin, and was entirely unknown to either the Hebrew or the Egyptian. But especially in its present use as designating the various powers, or attributes of the mind, it is a *modern* word exclusively. The ancients knew nothing of such a division of the mind, or soul into faculties. The presence, therefore, of this one word alone in the Book of Mormon is sufficient to prove that it is *not a translation* of the ancient Egyptian language, as no such word with such a meaning is found in that or any other ancient language.

The word "popular," on page 209. A certain mischief maker is represented as going about among the people declaring:

"That every priest and teacher ought to become popular; and they ought not to labor with their hands, but that they ought to be supported by the people."

"Popular" is also a Latin word from "*populos,*" meaning "*people.*" But in the sense in which it is used in this place, it is *entirely modern*. In fact, the whole sentence is modern in its conception, peculiarly so. It is, indeed, strange that the author could have so far lost his wits as to allow his anxiety to slap clergymen of the present day in the face, to lead him into a blunder that proves his work a fraud beyond a possibility of question. For over and over again the Book of Mormon declares that *Lehi* and his descendants *kept the law of Moses*, with the greatest carefulness, until Christ came who set aside the law by fulfilling it. So exact were they in this observance that Nephi and his people built a magnificent temple, patterned after the temple of Solomon, almost immediately upon their arrival in this country, and set apart their two youngest brothers as priests. Well now, one of the first and plainest requirements of the law of Moses was the setting apart of the tribe of Levi to the work of the priesthood, and the provision for their *complete and abundant support by a tax of one-tenth of all the income of the nation.*

But here in this paragraph a man gets himself into trouble and finally suffers the penalty of death for publicly teaching that "priests ought not to labor with their hands, *but be supported by the people,*" precisely the thing that the law of Moses absolutely and unconditionally required. Surely the writer of the above could not have been an ancient writer, but a *modern* man with a *very* strong desire to hit hard the *modern* custom of a *salaried* ministry.

In connection with this same sinner, on page 210, we have the word "priestcraft" three times repeated:

"Behold this is the first time that priestcraft has been introduced among this people. And behold, thou art not only guilty of priestcraft, but hast endeavored to enforce it by the sword; and were priestcraft to be enforced among this people, it would prove their entire destruction."

The word *"priest"* is old, and the word *"craft"* and "crafty" is old; but putting the two words together in the sense in which it is used here is a conception of modern times, growing out of the corruptions and the priestly power of the Church of Rome.

On page 227 we find the expression, "awful dilemma:"

* * * "That I should find that ye were not in the awful dilemma that our brethren were in at Zarahemla."

And again on the next page:

"I had much desire that ye were not in the state of dilemma like your brethren."

State of dilemma is not a correct use of the word. There is no such thing as a *state* of dilemma. But the word *dilemma* is from the Greek language, and has no counterpart, so far as I can find, in the Hebrew or the Egyptian language.

And still more than this may be said of the word *"synagogue,"* found in several places. For instance, on page 254:

"And Alma and Amulek went forth preaching repentance to the people in their temples, and in their sanctuaries, and also in their synagogues, which were built after the manner of the Jews."

This occurred, according to the chronology of the book, about one hundred and fifteen years before Christ visited this country in person. And the above statement shows that there were at that time *three kinds of buildings* used for religious purposes; *why* they needed so many kinds we are not informed. First, "temples;" second, "sanctuaries;" and third, "synagogues;" and these synagogues were "built *after the manner of the Jews.*"

Now, friends, seriously, how did those people, over one hundred years before Christ visited them, *find out about Jewish synagogues?*" The word itself is a *Greek* word, not found in any other ancient language; it is not found in the Old Testament. Indeed, as a matter of fact, no such places of worship were known to the Old Testament Jews. While the first temple was standing, the Jews had only the *one sanctuary.* The Egyptians had only *temples,* which were *national* and not *local places* of worship. No form of religion on earth had ever provided for or required local places of worship. It was not until after the *dispersion* of the Jews into various foreign countries, so remote from each other as to forbid a national gathering, that places of worship were built in each separate city or community, where the people could meet together on the Sabbath day to read and expound the law and the prophets. And these places were called *synagogues wherever the Greek language prevailed.* The word simply means a *"place of meeting."*

But no such places were known, and no such word as synagogue had ever been heard by Nephi and his people when they left Jerusalem and came to this country, six hundred years before Christ. And they had no communication with the old world, and probably never had heard of such a language as the Greek. Where, then, did they get the word *synagogue*, and especially where did they get the *model upon which to construct these buildings?*

Once more, let me read you a passage that, to say the least, is a very odd one to have been uttered nearly 600 years before Christ. On page 107:

"And my words shall hiss forth unto the ends of the earth, for a standard unto my people, which are of the house of Israel. And because my words shall hiss forth, many Gentiles shall say, a bible, a bible, we have got a bible, and there cannot be any more bible. But thus saith the Lord God; O fools, they shall have a bible; and it shall proceed forth from the Jews, mine ancient covenant people. And what thank they the Jews for the bible which they receive from them? * * * Thou fool that shall say a bible, we have got a bible, and we need no more bible. Have ye obtained a bible, save it were by the Jews? Know ye not that there are more nations than one?"

And then the author proceeds in the most approved Mormon style of the present day to argue the necessity of a continued and perpetual revelation, proving, if his arguments prove anything, that there should be a separate "bible" for every separate nation on earth:

"For behold I shall speak unto the Jews, and they shall write it; and I shall also speak unto the Nephites, and they shall write it; and I shall also speak unto the other tribes of the house of Israel, which I have led away, and they shall write it; and I shall also speak unto all the nations of the earth and they shall write it."

Utterly oblivious, apparently, of the fact that the very terms he uses expose the whole thing as a fraud of the first water.

The word "Bible," as applied to the Holy Scriptures, was never heard of or thought of until centuries after the Christian era. "*Hiera grammata*,"(*sacred writings*), was the term used in New Testament times to designate the various books that made up the Word of God. You, of course, understand that the books of the Bible were written separately and circulated separately for ages. It was nearly 200 years after Christ before the various books of the New Testament had been collected and, in connection with the books of the Old Testament, put together into one volume, to which was given still later the name, "*Ho Biblos*," the Greek word for *book* "*the Book*," from which, with an English termination, we get the word *Bible*. And yet this word that had no meaning whatever for at least 800 years after Nephi's time, is put into his mouth as glibly as it would be uttered to-day.

It is said in reply, that this is a *prophecy* of Nephi's; he is foretelling what Gentiles of to-day will say about the word of God. This does not meet the difficulty. All the prophecies of the Bible are uttered in the current language of the day, in the vernacular of the prophet who utters them. To suppose that Nephi, who uses the reformed Egyptian, should utter prophecies in the Greek, a language he had never heard of, would be simply preposterous. He would be talking *Chocktaw* both to himself and to all who listened to him, for this occurs in the midst of an earnest speech delivered to his "beloved brethren," who are standing around him. How absurdly ridiculous for Nephi to stand up before his brethren, all of whom are reformed Egyptian in speech, and say in his native tongue, "My beloved brethren, many of the Gentiles shall say, a *biblos*, a *biblos*, we have got a *biblos*, and we need no more *biblos!*"

Let me mention one other word several times used in the Book of Mormon: *"immortal,"* joined to the word *soul*, *"immortal soul,"* an expression that is not only modern in its use, not found in any of the ancient languages, not found in either the Old or New Testament,— but is, in fact, directly at variance with the plain statements of the New Testament. It is a popular expression of modern invention, designed to express a solemn Bible truth, but unfortunately puts into the word immortal a meaning that does not belong to it. Immortal means, "not subject to death." It is applied, in the Bible, to the *body after the resurrection*: but not applied to the soul here in this life, because the Bible expressly represents the soul of the sinner as *already dead* "in trespasses and in sins." It has no life, real true life, until it has been regenerated by the Spirit of God and made alive in Christ. Hence the word *immortal* is not a proper word to describe the soul here, for instead of being "not subject to death," it is already dead. The popular meaning of the word is that the soul shall never cease to exist, which is true; but the word immortal is not the right word to express that truth.

The use, then, of this word alone, as applied to the soul, in the Book of Mormon, would be an indisputable proof that the book is modern in its conception and make-up, and could not be from God, for God cannot contradict himself. He could not possibly be beguiled into the use of a word that would contradict the express teachings of the Bible.

There are many other words whose existence in the Book of Mormon proves its modern origin; as, the word "barges," the name given to Jared's vessels, or arks, nearly 2500 years before Christ. It is from the Danish *Bargie*.

The word "Jew" or "Jews," used on almost every page of the Book of Mormon, a *nickname* given to the scattered remnants of God's ancient people long after the Christian era, very improperly found in our English version of the New Testament, but not in the original Greek. In every instance the Greek says, *Ioudaioi* ("Judeans," or inhabitants of Judea).

"*Gentiles*," from the Latin *Gentilis*, a word absolutely without meaning to the Nephites and Lamanites in this country, who were all descendants of one family, the tribe of *Manassah*.

"Baptize," from the Greek, but used in this country 150 years before Christ as we use it to-day in the English to describe the Christian ordinance.

So the word "church," a modern word, from the Danish "kirke," or the German "kirche," put into the New Testament as the translation of the Greek word *ekklasia* (an *assembly*), but used in this country 150 years before Christ's time.

There are many words and phrases, usually called *slang* phrases, that are well known to be modern, and only modern, in their use, such as the word "hinderment," on page 250:

"And he became a great hinderment to the prosperity of the church."

The phrase "make game," on page 491:

"Yea, ye need not any longer hiss, nor spurn, nor make game of the Jews, nor any of the remnant of the house of Israel."

A slang phrase that is not only modern in its origin, but if I mistake not, originated in our own country.*

But why need I specify words, single words, when there are *sentences by the thousand, and whole chapters*, whose very presence in the Book of Mormon, in the form in which they are found, settles the question of the modern origin of the book beyond the possibility of question. I refer to all the quotations from the Bible, embracing, as I have already shown you, so large a part of the book. They are every one of them, with scarcely an exception, *made verbatim from our modern English version*, the King James' version of the Bible, made a little over 200 years ago.

You have all known this fact, of course, ever since you first knew the Book of Mormon. But I am convinced you have never carefully considered what that fact means, or you must have rejected it at once as a fraud. I need only repeat to you the manner of preparing the Book of Mormon as related by the eye witnesses.

David Whitmer states as follows:

"The tablets, or plates were translated by Smith, who used a small oval, or kidney-shaped stone, called Urim and Thummim, that seemed endowed with the marvelous power of converting the characters on the plates, when used by Smith, into English, who would then dictate to Cowdry what to write. Frequently one character would make two

---

*It has been replied to the argument from the use of all these modern words that "the angel who translated those ancient plates for Joseph Smith would be apt to use words with which Joseph Smith was familiar; he would clothe the ancient thought in a modern dress, and use such simple modern expressions as Joseph Smith, who was an unlettered man, could readily understand."

To this it is sufficient to reply that while this supposition, if true, might account for the existence of some of the words already mentioned in the Book of Mormon, such as "Jew," "baptism," "church," "popular," etc., words that may have had some counterpart in the ancient language in which those plates were written, it could by no possibility be made to account for the existence in the Book of Mormon of such words as "faculties," "synagogue," "Gentiles," "Bible," "immortal soul," "make game," and other words that, as we have seen, *had no counterpart* in any ancient language with which the Nephites had any knowledge.

lines of manuscript, while others made but a word or two words." — "Myth of the Manuscript Found," page 83.

Martin Harris explains the translation as follows:

"By the aid of the seer stone, sentences would appear and were read by the prophet and written by Martin, and when finished he would say, 'Written,' and if correctly written, that sentence would disappear and another appear in its place; but if not written correctly it remained until corrected, so that the translation was just as it was engraven on the plates, precisely in the language then used."—Myth of the M. F., page 91.

These two witnesses, you observe, exactly agree as to the *modus operandi*. Joseph Smith has one of the plates before him, and places this oval-shaped stone directly over one of the characters upon the plate; and the stone is endowed with the marvelous power of translating that character into the English language, so that Joseph Smith is permitted to read the English word or sentence as it appears on the top of the stone. You see the Egyptian character is underneath, and its English equivalent appears on top of the stone, so that there can be no posssible chance of mistake. Mr. Smith has simply to read the sentence as it appears on top of the stone, and Mr. Cowdry, seated at a short distance from Mr. Smith, with a blanket hung up between them, copies or writes each sentence as it falls from Mr. Smith's lips. And to prevent the possibility of mistake, the sentence or word *remains on the stone in full view of Mr. Smith until Mr. Cowdry has had time to write it out in full.* And if Mr. Cowdry for any reason misunderstands Mr. Smith, and thus makes a mistake, the sentence *will not down*, it still persists in remaining there until the mistake has been corrected. Neither Mr. Smith nor Mr. Cowdry have any responsibility in the matter, except, simply, the one to announce and the other to write down whatever appears on the top of the stone. If the sentences are awkwardly expressed, or grammatically incorrect, or contain useless verbiage, unnecessary repetitions, or have errors of doctrine, or blunders of any kind, it is not at all the fault of Mr. Smith or Mr. Cowdry; it must be charged to the stone, or the angel that works it, or to the original writing underneath the stone. These earnest men have only to announce and write down what the stone records.

And whether the sentence that appears on the top of the stone is really a translation of the characters under the stone, they have no possible means of knowing. Both are uneducated men and know nothing whatever of the Egyptian characters they are translating. All they know about it, and all they claim to know about it, is that an angel, or some celestial personage that looked like an angel, as they supposed, appeared to them and told them that the words on top of the stone were a translation true and faithful of the characters underneath.

It is claimed there are *eleven* witnesses to the credibility of the Book of Mormon. But it can be readily seen that not one of them is, or can be a credible witness. They saw the plates, some plates, and describe their size, general appearance, etc. But every witness fails, just at the point where an anxious world want information, that is whether those plates contain an incongruous lot of characters that represented nothing whatever, or were a genuine record; and if a genuine record, whether they contained the whole or any part of the Book of Mormon. In other words, whether Joseph Smith was honest or playing upon their credulity they had no possible means of knowing, farther than the statement of this redoubtable angel.

And now, friends, on the supposition that Joseph Smith was an honest, earnest man, I propose, by four plain and simple facts, to show you positively and conclusively *that this angel was a fraud.* That when he told Joseph Smith that the words which appeared to him on the top of that stone were a translation true and faithful of the characters on the plates underneath the stone, *he told a lie.*

1. As they proceed with their work of translating, the stone is placed upon a character, and behold, there appears on the top of the stone a passage from our Bible; and it is in the language of our King James' version, precisely as it was translated by the English bishops 200 years ago.

Now, that sentence on top of the stone is either a translation of the characters under the stone, or it is not. If it is a translation made under the authority and by the direction of an angel of God, then we are confronted with this wonderful phenomenon, *that the angel should translate exactly as those English bishops*, not varying in a single word, although there are several thousand whole verses of this character, thus stamping, as you see, with heaven's seal the work of those grand old bishops, proving that they were infallible, absolutely so, never having made a single mistake, the angel agreeing with them in every instance, even to the wording of their thoughts.*

---

*And the wonder will only be increased when we learn that all the quotations from the Old Testament made prior to the appearance of Christ here upon this continent—that is, all the direct Bible quotations found in the book from the first to the 450th page—are translated from original *brass plates engraved in the pure Egyptian language*; plates brought by Nephi from the city of Jerusalem 600 years before Christ,

Just think of it! Those bishops, 200 years ago, translated from a Hebrew text that has been handed down to us from generation to generation, copied and recopied a thousand times over, perhaps; and their translation from such a Hebrew text is found to accord exactly, even to the minutest particular, with a translation made by an angel direct from Egyptian plates 2600 years old; less one single transcription, and that made by the inspired prophet Mormon.—See pages 10, 11, 63 and 154.

But the scholarship of the world has over and over again declared that those men *were not infallible;* that they did make a large number of mistakes; no very serious ones it is true, nothing that changes any great doctrine of the Bible; but, nevertheless, faults enough to keep them humble, and show that they were only human. And if I mistake not, our Mormon friends, in their Articles of Faith, say, "We believe the Bible to be the word of God, *as far as it is translated correctly,*" intimating that it was not altogether translated correctly; whereas, the testimony of this stone and the angel is that the translation is absolutely perfect, without fault.

If, on the other hand, that passage appearing on the top of the stone is not a translation of the characters underneath the stone, but is simply quoted word for word from our Bible, *then the whole claim is proven false.* For if in *one instance* the sentence appearing on top of the stone does not represent perfectly and exactly the characters underneath—is not a bonfide *translation*, then the same thing might occur in a thousand instances; in fact, in every instance, so that the characters underneath the stone need have no connection whatever with the words that appear on top. In other words, if Joseph Smith, in several thousand instances, went outside of the plates underneath his stone for his sentences, went directly to our Bible and quoted from it, *what proof have we that he did not go outside of the plates for every other sentence found in the Book of Mormon?*

2. The *second* fact I wish to present in proof of the deception practiced by the angel is this: According to the testimony of the eye-witnesses, there were only plates enough to furnish about *one eighth or one tenth of the contents* of the Book of Mormon, *upon the most liberal estimate possible.*

Mr. Martin Harris describes the size of the plates. —See Myth of M. F., page 89:

"He pointed with one of the fingers of his left hand to the back of his right hand and said, 'I should think they were about so long,' or about eight inches."

The plates were, then, about eight inches long. Mr. Harris does not give their width, but they are understood to have been about *seven* inches wide.

The specimen of Egyptian words shown on page 71 will sufficiently illustrate a well known fact, that both the Egyptian hieroglyphics and their written words are, many of them, the large majority of them, large sprawling characters that occupy a great deal of space on a page. I suppose it would hardly be possible to get as much matter on a page of Egyptian characters as you could get on a page of ordinary *hand writing*. As compared with fine printed matter, such as is found in the Book of Mormon, it would probably require not less than four or five such plates to make one page of closely printed matter. .

But I remember those characters were not all *Egyptian;* the specimens copied for the examination of the outside world are said to be made up, in part, of Hebrew and Arabic characters, both of which are able to be written in a much smaller compass than the Egyptian. As printed from type, the Hebrew is capable of being compressed into nearly as small a compass as a printed page of English. Of course, when written by hand or engraven upon plates, it could hardly be put into so small a compass.

But for the sake of the argument, we will suppose one page of the plates could furnish material for a full page of closely set, small type, such as the Book of Mormon. There are 563 pages in the Book of Mormon, which would therefore require 563 plates; probably, 1500 would be far nearer the truth.

Let us now see if we can ascertain anything near the probable number of plates used. Mr. Harris is quoted as saying (See Myth of M. F., page 89.):

> "He pointed with one of the fingers of his left hand to the back of his right hand and said, 'I should think they were so long,' or about eight inches, 'and about so thick,' or about four inches; 'and each of the plates was thicker than the thickest tin.' "

This informs us that when these plates were laid together in a pile, they made a pile *about four inches thick;* and that each plate was *thicker than the thickest tin.* I called at a hardware store the other day, and with the help of a clerk, measured the thickness of some tin, not the thickest, but a little more than medium thickness; and we found it required *sixty plates of this tin to make one inch.* But Mr. Harris says these plates were *thicker* than the *thickest* tin. (They would need to be thus thick to form a sufficient body for the work of the engraver.) It would then be a very liberal estimate to suppose there were *fifty* of these plates to the inch, or a total of *200* plates in the pile of *four inches*—that is, plates enough to furnish material for 200 pages of the Book of Mormon.

But here is a witness who lets in a little more light. I read from Myth of M. F., page 82:

> "The plates which Mr. Whitmer saw were in the shape of a tablet, fastened with three rings, about one-third of which appeared to be loose in plates, the other solid, but with perceptible marks where the plates seemed to be sealed, and the guide that pointed it out to Smith very impressively reminded him that the loose plates alone were to be used, the sealed portion was not to be tampered with."

Several other testimonies are to the same effect. Mr. Harris, for instance, says (Ibid, page 88):

"And as many of the plates as Joseph Smith translated, I handled with my hands, plate after plate."

Instead, then, of having all the plates which together make a pile *four inches thick*, there were actually used only about *one-third* of the plates; the balance, or *two-thirds*, remained sealed up for future use. *One-third* of 200 plates would be sixty-six or sixty-seven plates; the total number, therefore, from which a book of 563 pages of closely printed matter was derived. Sixty-seven, instead of 563 plates, which is the *lowest possible estimate*, while 1500 is the more probable one.

3. But there is still a third statement in proof that the contents of the Book of Mormon did not come from the plates. It is the statement of Mr. David Whitmer already read that "frequently *one character would make two lines of manuscript*, while others made but a word or two words.

We can readily believe this statement. A man who could read several thousand verses from the King James' version of the Bible out of the characters on those plates, could easily read *two lines* of manuscript, or a *dozen lines*, if desired, from one character. But the above is an exceedingly unfortunate admission. It is true, as I tried to illustrate in the second lecture, that the Hebrew characters are often very expressive and comprehensive, frequently requiring two and three and possibly four words in our language to correctly translate one Hebrew character. But a man who has ever translated from any of the ancient languages would smile with credulity if you should tell him that "frequently one character would make two lines of manuscript," unless, indeed, the lines were *very short*, or the words wonderfully drawn out, so that three or four words at the most could occupy two full lines. It was simply impossible, friends, that one character could ever make two full lines of ordinary manuscript.

4. One other fact and I will close this examination for the present.

Let me read you again from the testimony of Martin Harris:

> "Martin Harris related an incident that occurred during the time that he wrote that portion of the translation of the Book of Mormon, which he was favored to write direct from the mouth of the Prophet Joseph Smith. He said that the Prophet possessed a seer stone, by which he was enabled to translate as well as from the Urim and Thummim, and for convenience he then used the seer stone."—Myth of the M. F., page 91.

It seems almost too bad that he should thus inadvertantly give the whole thing away. For you must understand that the Urim and Thummim spoken of, and called throughout the Book of Mormon "the Interpreters," had been provided with great care over 2500 year ago by God himself, for the express purpose of translating these plates. They are often mentioned in the Book of Mormon as exceedingly important. They were preserved with the greatest care, handed down from one generation to another with the plates, and buried with them in the hill Cumorah over 1400 years ago; as sacred as the plates themselves. So sacred that only one man was allowed to handle or use them, the highly favored prophet, Joseph Smith, himself. But now, alas! after all this trouble and pains and care on the part of God, and on the part of so many holy men of old, this "Urim and Thummim" is found at last to be *altogether superflous; not needed at all.* Martin Harris tells us that the Prophet Joseph Smith possessed a *"seer stone,"* a sort of *"peep stone,"* by which he was enabled to translate *as well* as from the Urim and Thummim; and, "*for convenience,* he used the seer stone." So we are left to infer that when he used the Urim and Thummim at all, it was at *some inconvenience.* And he probably only did it out of regard to the feelings of his God, who had spent so much time and anxiety in preparing it so long ago, and preserving it to the present day for his special use.

(The closing sentences of this lecture were left out after it had been decided to publish a fourth lecture.)

LECTURE IV.

(This lecture, in substance, was delivered by special request at the Walker Opera House, Sabbath Evening, July 26.)

"For my thoughts are not your thoughts, neither are your ways my ways, saith the Lord.

"For as the heavens are higher than the earth, so are my ways higher than your ways, and my thoughts than your thoughts."—Isaiah, 55: 8, 9.

1. A few of the *mistakes* of the Book of Mormon:

a. Some of the *types* presented in the Book of Mormon contradict the plain teachings of the Bible.

For instance, the Bible *type* for the word of God itself is *water, pure living* water. It is used thus, probably, in a hundred places. So complete is the type, that we are able to trace its likeness through nearly all the various uses of water.

Water is used for *cleansing purposes*, so the word of God.—See Psalms, 119: 9; 2nd Cor., 7: 1; 1st Peter, 1: 22; John, 17: 17, and 15: 3; Eph., 5: 26, 27, and others.

Water is used for *quenching thirst*, so the word of God.—See Isaiah, 55: 1; John, 7: 37, and 4: 10, 14, and 6: 35; Rev., 21: 6, and 22: 17, and others.

Water is used for *reviving nature*, so the word of God.—See Isaiah, 55: 10, 11; Ezk., 47: 1-12; Psalms, 1: 2, 3; 1st Cor., 3: 6, compared with Acts, 18: 24, 28.

Now please bear in mind, friends, that God never uses a word by chance, never puts a word in simply to fill up, or round out a sentence as we often do. Every type chosen is carefully and wisely chosen. And God never mixes things, never confuses by using a typical word in a variety of senses, making it mean one thing in one passage and another thing in another passage. If pure living water is found to be a type of the word of God in one passage, then we have found a *key* that will unlock every passage where pure living water is used in a typical sense. It always means the word of God, never anything else.

But on page 20, Nephi, 3: 17, we have this statement:

"And it came to pass that I beheld that the rod of iron which my father had seen, was the word of God, which led to the fountain of living waters, or to the tree of life; which waters are a representation of the love of God; and I also beheld that the tree of life was a representation of the love of God."

At least *three* errors in this one sentence. *1*. He makes a rod of iron a type of the word of God, and repeats the same statement on page 31. *2*. He makes living water a type of the *love* of God, and then: *3*. Immediately mixes types by saying that the tree of life represents the love of God.

But upon page 32, he changes his mind as to the meaning of water:

"And they said unto me, what meaneth the river of water which our father saw? And I said unto them that the water which my father saw was filthiness: and so much was his mind swallowed up in other things that he beheld not the filthiness of the water."

Think of it! A man inspired by the Holy Spirit and helped constantly by an angel of God having his mind so much "swallowed up in other things" that he entirely mistakes the character of the water which he saw; and it is left for this young son of his, inspired by the same spirit and helped by the same angel, to *correct his father's mistake.*

But the young man, Nephi, has a very fruitful mind. After telling us that the river of water meant filthiness, immediately concludes he has not yet exhausted his subject and therefore adds:

"And I said unto them, that it, (this river of water), was an awful gulf which separated the wicked from the tree of life, and also from the saints of God."

Now, friends, to the careful student of the Bible, who learns how exceedingly careful its statements, how wisely chosen, and then how uniformly adhered to from Genesis to Revelations, are its types and symbols, this one instance of mixture and change and uncertainty is sufficient to brand the book as a fraud, when it pretends to have come from the all wise and unchangeable God.

b. The Bible tells us plainly and positively that the Holy Spirit as a person, the third person in the Godhead, was not given to the world until Jesus himself had come in the flesh and accomplished his mission. The Holy Spirit is sometimes mentioned in the Old Testament. His work in the creation of the world is alluded to in the very first chapter of Genesis; his work in inspiring the Old Testament scriptures is positively stated in 2nd Peter, 1: 21. But his work *was not understood by the Old Testament saints.* As Jesus was actively at work all through the Old Testament history, was in fact the Jehovah, the Lord of the Old Testament, but was not known as a separate and distinct personality, not revealed as the only begotten son, till he came here in the flesh; so the Holy Spirit, though actively at work, was not known as a separate person, his real office and work were not understood, until the dispensation of the spirit was ushered in on the day of Pentacost, and he was revealed in his fullness of blessing. In fact, the *third* person could not be revealed to men *before* the *second* person, the Lord Jesus, had been manifested. Upon this point, the statements of the New Testament are very plain and positive:

"But this spake he of the spirit, which they that believe on him should receive: for the Holy Ghost was not yet given; because that Jesus was not yet glorified."—John, 7: 39.

A very positive statement that the "Holy Ghost was not yet given," and the reason stated, "because that Jesus was not yet glorified." Peter, on the day of Pentacost, says expressly:

"Therefore, being by the right hand of God exalted, and having received of the Father the promise of the Holy Ghost, he hath shed forth this which ye now see and hear,"—Acts, 2: 33; see verses 16 and 18.

Equally conclusive are the words of the Savior:

"Nevertheless I tell you the truth; it is expedient for you that I go away; for if I go not away, the Comforter will not come unto you; but if I depart, I will send him unto you."—John, 16: 7; see also John, 14: 16, 26; and 15: 26; and 16: 13.

Well now, in the face of these positive statements of the New Testament, hear what Nephi says nearly 600 years before Christ. After telling his people, in prophecy, of the baptism of the Lord Jesus, and the Holy Ghost descending upon him in the form of a dove, he adds, (Pages 110, 111; 2nd Nephi, 13: 2-5.):

"And also the voice of the son came unto me saying, he that is baptized in my name, to him will the Father give the Holy Ghost, like unto me.

* * * "Yea, by following your Lord and Savior down into the water, according to his word, behold then shall ye receive the Holy Ghost; yea, then cometh the baptism of fire and of the Holy Ghost, and then can ye speak with the tongue of angels, and shout praises unto the Holy One of Israel.

* * * "Yea, ye have entered in by the gate: ye have done according to the commandments of the Father and the Son; and ye have received the Holy Ghost, which witnesseth of the Father and the Son."

And such statements are over and over again repeated all through the book, with all the accompanying extraordinary gifts that followed the day of Pentacost, and many more:

"Yea, having been favoured above every other nation, kindred, tongue and people; having been visited by the spirit of God; having conversed with angels, and having been spoken unto by the voice of the Lord; and having the spirit of prophecy, and the spirit of revelation and also many gifts: the gift of speaking with tongues, and the gift of preaching, and the gift of the Holy Ghost, and the gift of translation, etc.— Page 234; Alma, 7: 2.

In his desire to " beat the Bible," and exalt his pet Nephites to Heaven with privileges that no other people on earth possessed, our author should have been careful, and not so flatly contradict the plain statements of the New Testament, which he professes to receive with all reverence as the word of God.

c. King Jacob tells us on page 120, that a "hundredth part of the proceedings of this people, which now began to be numerous, cannot be written upon these plates; but many of their proceedings are written upon the larger plates, and their wars and their contentions and the reigns of their kings."

Fifty-five years before this statement, Jacob's father, Lehi, left Jerusalem with his wife and four boys, all unmarried. Another family, consisting of Ishmael and wife, two sons and several daughters, were induced to accompany them. One other man, Zerum, who had been a slave of Laban, made up the total outfit.

During the first ten years, those four boys and the slave appear to have married those girls, while two other boys, Jacob and Joseph, are added to the original family of Lehi. If during the next ten years each of the five young families multiply as rapidly as possible, we cannot count more than from 30 to 40 young children, and during the next ten years the third decade, the largest possible increase would not reach 50 more children. So that at the end of *thirty* years we have twelve grown people and from 75 to 90 children—of whom there are possibly from 10 to 15 who have reached the age of 20 years, and may possibly have intermarried.

And friends, it was during this last decade, between twenty and thirty years after leaving Jerusalem, probably about twenty-two or twenty-three years after, when there was a possible population of between 50 and 60 persons, nearly all of whom are small children, that this company divide into *two nations*. The two oldest brothers, Laman and Lemuel, with their families, and the two sons of Ishmael, under the general designation of *Lamanites*, remain in South America, and elect a king! while the balance, under the direction of Nephi, at the command of God, strike off into the wilderness in the direction of North America, choose Nephi as their king, and assume the name of Nephites!—and before the first thirty years have expired, that is in about seven or eight years, this little colony have subdued the forests, become wealthy in flocks and herds, been taught by Nephi to

"Build buildings; and to work in all manner of wood, and of iron, and of copper, and of brass, and of steel (?), and of gold and of silver, and of precious ores, which were in great abundance."

And in addition to all this, he had built and completed a *temple:*

"And I did construct it after the manner of the temple of Solomon, save it were not built of so many precious things; for they were not to be found upon the land*; wherefore, it could not be built like unto Solomon's temple. But the manner of the construction was like unto the temple of Solomon; and the workmanship thereof was exceeding fine."

Pretty good for three men and a few boys! Solomon's temple was *seven* years in building, and required 153,000 laborers and 30,000 overseers—see 1st Kings 5: 13-16, and 6: 37-38.

After the completion of this magnificent temple, Nephi consecrates his two youngest brothers, Jacob and Joseph, though now scarcely more than twenty years old, to the office of the priesthood:

"And it came to pass that I, Nephi, did consecrate Jacob and Joseph that they should be priests and teachers over the land† of my people."

In doing this he directly broke two very plain requirements of the Mosaic law. 1. That none but the tribe of Levi were eligible to the priesthood—these men being from the tribe of *Mannaseh.* 2. That no one should be permitted to discharge the duties of a priest till *thirty years of age.* We should remember, however, that this small nation had but little timber as yet to

---

* He has *all manner* of wood, iron, copper, brass, steel, gold, silver, and precious ores in great abundance: precisely what " precious things " he needed aside from all these, does not clearly appear.

† They certainly had plenty of *land* to be priests and teachers over, but the people were scarce.

select from. Nephi himself was king and general high priest—his brother Samuel and the slave Zerum were the subjects, and so these two boys, Jacob and Joseph, were all there were left for priests except the small children who had been born within the two previous decades.

And friends, it is during the next twenty-five years that these two imposing nations, the Nephites and the Lamanites, had so many wars and contentions, shed so much blood, and made so much history, that Jacob tells us in the passage above quoted that

"A hundredth part of the proceedings of this people cannot be written upon these plates! and that many of their proceedings are written upon the larger plates, and their wars, and their contentions, and the reigns of their kings."

A love of the marvellous, combined with a somewhat stoical indifference to the ridiculous, must surely have been a prominent and important factor in the mental make-up of our author!

d. On page 139, Omni. 1: 6, 7, we are told of a party of Nephites, under the leadership of one Mosiah, who fled out of their own land, and, after wandering a long time through the wilderness, discovered a land called the land of Zarahemla, inhabited by a people who came out from Jerusalem only a few years after Lehi and his company; and, like Lehi, had been brought by the hand of the Lord across the great waters, and had settled on this continent, and increased until they had become a numerous and wealthy people. And please note the following statement:—

And they (Mosiah and his company) discovered a people who were called the people of Zarahemla. Now there was great rejoicings among the people of Zarahemla; and also Zarahemla (the king) did rejoice exceedingly because the

Lord had sent the people of Mosiah with the plates of brass which contained the record of the Jews."

In the very next section the author, evidently forgetting what he had just said, flatly contradicts it:

"And at the time Mosiah discovered them * * their language had become corrupted; and they had brought no records with them; and they denied the being of their Creator; and Mosiah nor the people of Mosiah could understand them."

In the first sentence Zarahemla and his people rejoice because the *Lord* had sent this party of strangers to them. In the next sentence we are told that Zarahemla and his people "*denied the being of their Creator.*"

In the first sentence we are still farther informed that the special reason of their rejoicing was because Mosiah and his company *had brought the brass plates* containing the record of the Jews.

In the next sentence we are told that their *language* had become *so corrupted that neither Mosiah nor his people could understand them!*

Friends, do you think this part of the Book of Morman was inspired of God?

There are other discrepancies and contradictions that can be explained upon no other theory so charitable as to suppose that the author had a poor memory, or else that his love of the marvellous ran away with his judgment, and sometimes even with his regard for the truth. For an instance of real bold lying, lying that has a wicked purpose in it, see page 25*. But the limits of

---

*Reference is had to the statement, four or five times repeated on the one page, that after the Apostles' day, a great and abominable church "took away from the Gospel of the Lamb of God many parts which are plain and most precious; and also many covenants of the Lord." In other words, that by the authority of the church, after the time of the Apostles, or some time after the first century, the Bible had much that was valuable—"the plain and most precious parts" taken away from it; so much eliminated that "an exceedingly great many do stumble,"etc. In this unfounded, malicious statement, the author shows himself as utterly devoid of principle as he was ignorant of the plainest facts of history. It is susceptible of the clearest proof that since the first century *not a chapter* has been taken out of the Bible.

this lecture will not allow a farther consideration of this first point.

---

2. I wish, in the second place, briefly to call attention to the peculiar character of the so called *prophecies* of the Book of Mormon. *They are put in the precise language that records their fulfillment.* A most singular and unheard of phenomenon! You will best understand me by noting a few specimens out of the hundreds that are found in the book. Nephi gives us the following specimen of his father Lehi's prophesying (Page 17; Nephi, 3: 3, 5):

"Yea, even 600 years from the time that my father left Jerusalem, a prophet would the Lord God raise up among the Jews; even a Messiah; or in other words, a Savior of the world.

"And he spake also concerning a prophet who should come before the Messiah, to prepare the way of the Lord; yea, even he should go forth and cry in the wilderness, prepare ye the way of the Lord, and make his paths straight; for there standeth one among you whom ye know not; and he is mightier than I, whose shoe's latchet I am not worthy to unloose. And much spake my father concerning this thing.

"And my father said he should baptize in Bethabara beyond Jordan * * * and after he had baptized the Messiah with water, he should behold and bear record that he had baptized the Lamb of God, who should take away the sin of the world."

Afterwards, Nephi himself prophecies after this fashion (Pages 20, 21):

"And I beheld the redeemer of the world of whom my father had spoken; and I also beheld the prophet who should prepare the way before him. And the Lamb of God went forth and was baptized of him; and after he was baptized, I beheld the heavens open, and the Holy Ghost came down out of heaven and abode upon him in the form of a dove.

"And he spake unto me again saying, look! and I looked and I beheld multitudes of people who were sick, and who were afflicted with all manner of diseases, and with devils and unclean spirits; and they were healed by the power of the Lamb of God.

"And I looked, and beheld the Lamb of God, that he was taken by the people * * * and I, Nephi, saw that he was lifted up upon the cross and slain for the sins of the world."

And thus I might quote hundreds of passages relating to Christ, telling his name, his mother's name, his place of residence, his reputed father's name, the particulars of his life and death, and the after history of the church as related in the New Testament, or revealed in the book of Revelations, very much of it *in the exact language of the New Testament.* And the same thing is true of the prophecies that relate to the present time. All about Joseph Smith, his name, his father's name, how he shall find those old plates, the witnesses who shall see them, the "spokesman," Sidney Rigdon, provided to aid him, etc., etc., all with as much particularity and minuteness of detail as though the prophecies had all been gotten up *after the events had transpired*, AS THEY UNDOUBTEDLY WERE.

And, indeed, it seems strange that the originators of the Book of Mormon were not sharp enough to cover up their fraud a little more carefully, but furnish upon almost every page the materials for their exposure.

How different the prophecies of the Bible. Any approach to *exact literalness* is apparently studiously avoided. The greater portion of the Old Testament prophecies that relate to Christ are in *types*; the old tabernacle and temple, its priesthood and their work, and the entire system of bloody sacrifices of meat and drink offerings, are all prophecies of Christ and the Christian dispensation.

Another common method of revealing the future is by symbol. A good illustration of this method was presented in the second lecture. The four beasts seen by the prophet Daniel presented in a remarkably brief compass a prophetic outline of the history of the four leading nations of the world for a period of over two thousand years. A large part of the Book of Revelations is occupied with this style of prophesying, so is Ezekiel. In fact, this method abounds in all the prophecies of the Bible. I can recall but one single instance in the Bible where a man's name is given prophetically. The Persian king, *Cyrus*, was called by name, by the prophet Isaiah, nearly 100 years before his birth. But this kind of literalness is the exception. John the Baptist's prophetic name was Elijah or Elias. Even Jesus, himself, is not mentioned by name in any of the Old Testament prophecies. Good old Jacob called him "Shiloh;" the prophet Zechariah named him the "Branch;" another, the "Rose of Sharon," the "Lily of the Valley," the "Lord our Righteousness," the "Sun of Righteousness," etc.

But in the Book of Mormon, Jesus' first announcement of himself in this country, one hundred years after the flood, runs thus:

"Behold I am he who was prepared from the foundation of the world to redeem my people; behold I am Jesus Christ, I am the Father and the Son."

The most literal prophecy in the Old Testament relating to Christ is the fifty-third chapter of Isaiah. Let me read you a portion of the verses:

1. "Who hath believed our report? and to whom is the arm of the Lord revealed?
2. "For he shall grow up before him as a tender plant, and as a root out of a dry ground; he hath no form nor comeliness; and when we shall see him, there is no beauty that we should desire him.
3. "He is despised and rejected of men; a man of sorrows, and acquainted with grief: and we hid as it were our faces from him; he was despised, and we esteemed him not.
7. "He was oppressed, and he was afflicted; yet he opened not his mouth; he is brought as a lamb to the slaugh-

ter, and as a sheep before her shearers is dumb, so he openeth not his mouth.

9. "And he made his grave with the wicked, and with the rich in his death, because he had done no violence, neither was any deceit in his mouth."

And do you know, friends, that although this chapter was never called in question by the Jews before Christ came, yet after he had lived and died, and had fulfilled both in his life and death so exactly and perfectly every statement made in this chapter, such is their hatred of the Savior that many Jews, even to the present day, have tried to persuade themselves that this one chapter has been interpolated into their sacred books. And infidels, too, from the very beginning of the Christian era to our own day, have exhausted every means in their power to write that one chapter out of the prophecies of Isaiah, and persuade themselves *it must have been written after* the events, so plainly foretold, had occurred. And yet, the evidence is abundant that that chapter, with all the rest of the book, was in existence just as we now find it, at least 200 years *before* Christ came in the flesh. The translation of the Old Testament Hebrew into the Greek lauguage, at Alexandria, Egypt, two hundred years before Christ, and the preservation of that translation by channels widely diverse and wholy independent of the original Hebrew, furnishes evidence that the scholarship of the world has never been able to successfully refute.

But now suppose this fifty-third chapter of Isaiah had been written after this fashion:

"I, Isaiah, a prophet of the Lord, and inspired by an angel from heaven, do hereby declare unto you, my beloved brethren, that in just 712 years from this date, a virgin by the name of Mary, living in the city of Nazareth, shall give birth to a son, whose name shall be Jesus Christ, the Lamb of God, the Savior of the world. This child, Jesus Christ, shall live until thirty years old with his reputed father, Joseph by name, and a carpenter by trade. At the age of thirty, he shall find his forerunner, John the Baptist, at a place called Bethabara, beyond the river Jordan, baptizing by immersion all who come to him. After Jesus is baptized, the heavens shall be opened, and the Holy Ghost shall be seen descending in bodily shape like a dove and resting upon him, and a voice from heaven shall be heard saying, this is my beloved son, hear ye him. After his baptism, he shall enter upon his public ministry, calling twelve men to be with him, whom he shall name apostles, and one of whom shall bear the name of John, and shall write a book that shall be called the Apocalypse, etc., etc."

Had we found this one chapter of Isaiah thus written, in language and style entirely different from every other chapter in the book, without a trace of the ancient Hebrew preserved, but instead, an exact reproduction of the New Testament Greek, idioms and all; do you think any sane man on earth could be found willing to accept it as a genuine production of the prophet Isaiah?

But let us go a step further in the supposed case. Suppose this chapter, written in the style just suggested, is a *modern discovery* altogether. A man in our day professes to have found some ancient writings engraven upon old plates. The discoverer is an ignorant man, knows nothing of either ancient or modern languages, and hence, has no possible means of knowing whether these plates he has found contain real ancient writings or simply unmeaning scrawls that somebody has scratched upon those plates for their own amusement, or for the express purpose of imposing upon his credulity and ignorance. And suppose our discoverer carefully and studiously keeps those plates hid from the public eye, refuses to allow a single scholar to examine them, or any person at all competent to judge of their real character, but claims that an angel from heaven is directing him in the matter.

And by and by there is published to the world a pretended translation of those plates, stating that the said plates *are a part of the original book of Isaiah, the prophet;* that a *lost chapter* is now restored to the world by the help of an angel of God.

But upon examination, this pretended lost chapter, translated by this ignorant man, helped by his angel, is found to be made up exclusively from our present English version of the New Testament, copied word for word from the history of Jesus Christ as we now have it recorded by Matthew, Mark, Luke and John—a feat that any Sunday-school scholar of ordinary intelligence could perform without any inspiration from God, or special help from an angel. Such prophecies can be manufactured to order by the cart load. And yet precisely this is the character of a *large portion* of the prophecies of the Book of Mormon. And you and I, friends, are asked to believe that such a silly and transparent fraud is from God.

---

3. In the third and last place, I desire briefly to call attention to a few of the *reputed* miracles of the Book of Mormon. Several were mentioned in the third lecture:

a. The first to be mentioned this evening occurred in immediate connection with the separation between Nephi and his two brothers, Laman and Lemuel, and the organization of the two infant but rival nations already referred to, between twenty and thirty years after leaving Jerusalem.

The miracle is certainly one of the most remarkable of the ages, settling one of the mooted questions of four-hundred years standing: "*How came the American In-*

dian with a black skin?" (The American Indian is the reputed descendant of the Lamanites.)

Nephi tells us that his two brothers, with their families, because of their opposition to Nephi, and their general depravity, became the subjects of a *peculiar curse.* —Page 66, 2nd Nephi, 4: 4:

"For behold they had hardened their hearts against him, that they had become like unto a flint; wherefore as they were white, and exceeding fair and delightsome, that they might not be enticing unto my people, the Lord God did cause a skin of blackness to come upon them. And thus saith the Lord God, I will cause that they shall be loathsome unto thy people, save they shall repent of their iniquities. And cursed shall be the seed of him that mixeth with their seed; for they shall be cursed even with the same cursing. And the Lord spake it and it was done."

It is strange what peculiar favorites of Heaven this Nephi and his people were, that God should be willing, for the sole purpose of removing temptation from them, "that they might not be enticing unto my people," to curse his own brothers with a skin of blackness. It is something God never did for any other people under heaven. He never exhibited such tender care for the *Jews* in all the Old Testament history. The New Testament furnishes no incidents of this character. The early Christians, in their best and purest days, had no such favors shown them. And, so far as we can learn, the Lord has never "caused a skin of blackness to come upon" any Gentile of modern times, to prevent their "becoming enticing to my people," the Latter-day Saints. All God's other saints, in all the ages, have been left to *grapple with temptations.* The notion somehow has pervaded the divine mind that strong temptations and fiery trials were needful to strengthen the faith and purify the life of his people; and, therefore, he has allowed his people—all his other people except these

Nephites—to meet sin face to face with all its blandishments; to live among and mingle freely with those who were "white and exceeding fair and delightsome," without any such tender precaution as to turn their temptors' skin black and make them loathsome, least his dear people should be coaxed into sin by their enticements!

If there could be anything more silly or preposterous than this, it is found on page 436, Nephi, 1: 9, occurring over five hundred years after the above:

> "And it came to pass that those Lamanites who had united with the Nephites were numbered among the Nephites, and their curse was taken from them, and their skin became white like unto the Nephites; and their young men and their daughters became exceeding fair, and they were numbered among the Nephites, and were called Nephites."

Wonderful! Wonderful! When a *black* man is soundly converted and unites himself with the people of God, the curse is removed, and he becomes white like the Nephites! Is'nt it so? Certainly, God is no respecter of persons. He is not partial in the bestowment of his favors. Would he remove the curse once, and in one portion of the world, and never do it again? Why, then, in all the history of the world was such a phenonema never heard of, that the color of the skin was changed in conversion? Have the unfortunate colored people anywhere on earth, in all the history of the past, been made white by conversion? Ah! but I forget. In the estimation of our Mormon friends there have been no true conversions since the first century after Christ until now. But in the very first age of the Church there were multitudes of the *Ethiopians* converted. Do you think the eunuch became white after Phillip baptized him? And now, in the last days, since the *fullness of the Gospel* has been restored to the earth by the Latter-day Saints, and scores and hundreds from the Indian races, the colored people, Asiatics, Sandwich Islanders, &c., have been soundly and thoroughly converted, has the skin of any of these converts been made white by the change any farther than soap and water would whiten them? Friends, produce your specimens, show us one single instance of the bleaching power of conversion upon the skin, or else hang your heads for shame, that you have allowed yourself to believe that such silly twaddle as this could be the word of Him who is *the same yesterday, to-day, and for ever*.

b. A little affair, too unimportant to be noticed, were it not that it flatly contradicts a rule which the world in general, and all biblical scholars in particular, have taken for granted without a question, because it so fully accords, not only with human reason and common sense, but with all the examples of the Bible, and all the records of God's dealings with his people. The rule is this: In the performance of a miracle, *God never does for us what we can do for ourselves.* He cultivates self-reliance and independence to that degree that he always employs human agency, human hands, and human brains, as far as they can be employed; and the divine aid comes in only where the *utmost of human effort fails to reach.* All that man can do he is expected to do. God only does for us what we cannot do for ourselves. But upon page 37, Nephi, 5:21, we have this statement:

"And after I had made a bellows that I might have wherewith to blow the fire, I did smite two stones together, that I might make fire; for the Lord had not hitherto suffered that we should make much fire, as we journeyed in the wilderness; for he said, I will make thy food become sweet, that ye cook it not; and I also will be your light in the wilderness."

I think comment upon this is not needful. There

was no lack of wood for fire in the wilderness, no lack of stones to smite together, but simply to prove to them that they are the Lord's special pets, he saves them the trouble of making fire by performing the prodigious miracle of making raw meat sweet and palatable, and of furnishing them light in the wilderness for their evening entertainments!

Of a similar character is a little occurrence related just before, page 35. It is usually supposed that a little common sense would be sufficient to tell a man who had spent some time traveling in a wild, mountainous region, about where he would naturally go to find wild game, if he wishes to hunt. But Nephi's God is so unusually good to him, that he takes the trouble to write the directions upon the pointers in a certain bal', called the "Director," (and which I will presently explain):

"And I said unto my father, whither shall I go to obtain food? And it came to pass that I did enquire of the Lord.
" * * * And it came to pass that the voice of the Lord said unto me, look upon the ball, and behold the things which are written. * * * And it came to pass that I, Nephi, did go forth up into the top of the mountain, according to the directions which were given upon the ball. And it came to pass that I did slay wild beasts, insomuch that I did obtain food for our families: and it came to pass that I did return* to our tents, bearing the beasts which I had slain."

c. But let me tell you about this strange ball, page 33:

"And it came to pass that the voice of the Lord spake unto my father by night, and commanded him that on the morrow he should take his journey into the wilderness. And it came to pass, that as my father arose in the morning and went forth to the tent door, to his great astonishment he beheld upon the ground, a round ball of curious work-

---

* Was the help of an angel needed to tell us that he returned to his tent after a successful hunt? Would God lumber his book with statements that a writer of ordinary intelligence would take for granted without recording.

manship, and it was of fine brass. And within the ball were two spindles; and the one pointed the way whither we should go into the wilderness."

And they start into the wilderness, "following the directions of the ball, which led us in the more fertile parts of the wilderness."

Here, friends, is a round ball, made of fine brass, and within it are two spindles, one of which points out constantly "the way whither we should go into the wilderness." Just how they could see spindles inside of a round brass ball, does not appear. However, as it was of *curious* workmanship, this may have been one of the curious things about it, we will therefore pass this as an unexplained wonder.

But those two spindles within this ball are the real puzzles. The author calls them *spindles* here, but on the next page he calls them *pointers*. Either word would indicate that they must have been small affairs, not capable of holding a very large amount of reading matter. But see page 35:

"And it came to pass that I, Nephi, beheld the pointers which were in the ball, that they did work according to the faith, and diligence, and heed which we did give unto them. And there was also written upon them a new writing, which was plain to be read, which did give us understanding concerning the ways of the Lord; and it was written and changed from time to time, according to the faith and diligence which we gave unto it. And thus we see that by small means the Lord can bring about great things."

Nephi's God certainly had an eye to convenience in this cute little affair. He had usually taken the trouble to send an angel down from heaven, or come himself, to inform Nephi and his father as to his will, from time to time. But by this ingenious mechanical device he saves himself any further trouble in that direction. One of the spindles points out the general directions they are to travel, and the other one (possibly both) has written upon it directions for special occasions, as for instance, where Nephi shall find a *deer*, or a *bear*, or a *wild turkey*, when the company are in want of food; the directions being "changed from time to time, according to the faith and diligence which we gave unto it. And thus we see that by small means the Lord can bring about great things." Yea, verily.

d. While upon this subject of ingenious inventions, let me call your attention to another, called a *compass*, also prepared of the Lord, which had the peculiar quality of *becoming balky and refusing to work* when anything was done against the Lord's pet, Nephi.

After wandering in the wilderness about eight years altogether, Nephi, at the command of God, builds a ship, and the whole party embark in it, with provisions, etc., to last them during a trip across the Indian and Pacific Oceans, until they shall land upon the shores of the new world, their promised land. Everything moves smoothly for a time; for the "space of many days they were driven forth before the wind towards the promised land." But by and by, a mutiny on ship board! Nephi preaches, and his two older brothers don't like his preaching. But please read page 42, III Nephi, 5: 37-42:

"And it came to pass, that Laman and Lemuel did take me and bind me with cords, and they did treat me with much harshness.

"And it came to pass that after they had bound me, insomuch that I could not move, the compass which had been prepared of the Lord did cease to work, wherefore they knew not whither they should steer the ship, insomuch* that there arose a great storm, yea a great and terrible tempest, and were driven back upon the waters for the space of three days,

---

* Just how their inability to steer the ship produced this terific storm is not explained. Probably the author mistook the meaning of *insomuch.*

and they began to be frightened exceedingly, least they should be drowned in the sea; nevertheless they did not loose me.

"And it came to pass that we were about to be swallowed up in the depths of the sea. And after we had been driven back upon the sea for the space of four days, my brethren began to see that the judgments of God were upon them, and that they must perish, save that they should repent of their iniquities; wherefore they came unto me and loosed the bonds which were upon my wrists.

"And it came to pass after they had loosed me, behold I took the compass and it did work whither I desired it. And it came to pass that I prayed unto the Lord; and after I had prayed the winds did cease, and the storm did cease, and there was a great calm."

Now, friends, do not think me a natural fault-finder, or a cavailler; but how can any intelligent mind read this without desiring to ask a few questions? And, first, I am slightly puzzled over this binding of Nephi with cords by his brothers. They had tried that thing on at least *three times* before with very unusual results.

On page 7, as these two older brothers began to smite Nephi with a rod, suddenly an angel of the Lord appeared upon the scene and said, "Why do ye smite your younger brother with a rod? Know ye not that the Lord hath chosen him to be ruler over you, and this because of your iniquities?"

On page 13, they became so enraged at his preaching that they bound him with cords, proposing to leave him in the wilderness, to be devoured by wild beasts; and he simply prayed unto the Lord, and suddenly "the bonds were loosed from my hands and feet, and I stood before my brethren and spake unto them again."

On page 40, as they were about to lay hands upon him, and throw him into the sea, he coolly straightened up and said to them:

"In the name of the Almighty God, I command you that ye touch me not, for I am filled with the power of God, even unto the consuming of my flesh; and whosoever shall lay hands upon me, shall wither even as a dried reed; and he shall be as naught before the power of God, for God shall smite him."

And the brothers' wicked purposes immediately collapsed:

"Neither durst they lay their hands upon me, nor touch me with their fingers, even for the space of many days, least they should wither before me."

But in a few days after this, the climax of absurdity is reached; the Lord is represented as removing this terrible ban, "raising the blockade" as it were, on this withering business, by introducing the following silly and childish expedient (page 41):

"And it came to pass, that the Lord said unto me, stretch forth thine hand unto thy brothers, and they shall not wither before thee, but I will shock them, saith the Lord, and this will I do, that they may know that I am the Lord their God. And it came to pass that I stretched forth my hand unto my brethren and they did not wither before me, but the Lord did shake them even according to the word which he had spoken. And now, they said, we know of a surety that the Lord is with thee; for we know that it is the power of the Lord that hath shaken us. And they fell down before me, and were about to worship me, but I would not suffer them, saying worship the Lord thy God, and honor thy father and thy mother."

But now, after all these experiences of the past, and this that he records upon these plates, you remember, is not a hundredth part of the things that actually occurred; probably, upon "mine other plates" would be found a hundred such incidents as this; and yet, after all this, we are asked to believe that these unnatural and strangely perverse brothers still venture to bind this chosen favorite of heaven, and that this time they succeed. No angel appears to rebuke them, no shock is felt when they touch him, no withering of limb or muscle; they bind him so tight that he cannot move, and the cords are not suddenly broken; he remains in their power for four long days. But, lo! instead of all these past experiences, an unexpected and unheard of phenomenon occurs! Their trusted compass, without which they are lost at sea, refuses to work, all on Nephi's account; and suddenly a terrible storm arises. Nature, herself, proposes to show her spite for the insult offered to this peculiar favorite of the gods. And this storm continues and increases its fury day and night, until, frightened out of their wits, and threatened with immediate death, these wicked brothers are forced once more to terms, and unloose their brother. Whereupon the storm ceases at once, and the compass resumes its wonted fidelity.

And what, friends, has been accomplished by all this reversal of nature's laws and angry exhibition of the tempest? In all the Bible examples of miraculous interposition, there is some important end to be gained, an end worthy the character and the dignity of the great God. But what has been gained in this case? An exhibition of spite on the part of Nephi, and whipping into submission those irate and foolish brothers.

Nephi evidently designs in this narrative to "pose" as a saint of the first water, but look at the facts as he himself states them. His wife and babes were pleading and crying with tears day and night, and his poor old father and mother were so overcome by the excitement and the excessive strain of the four days' terrific storm that they were prostrated, and brought down to death's door; and, in fact, the whole company are about to be swallowed up in the angry sea; and yet this man, Nephi, not only refuses to pray and thus bring about a great calm, but he coolly occupies his holy soul in spiritual exercises, for he says, "Nevertheless, I did look unto my God, and I did praise him all the day long." As much as to say to his brothers, "Now I have got you, and we will see who will beat this time! Let the old folks die, and wife and babies cry, it will not disturb my peace so long as I can whip you into submission by the help of this storm and the balky compass! When you say 'quits,' and unloose me, then I will pray and fix this thing up, but not till then!"

But a word about that compass. It is exceedingly puzzling to ascertain what it was good for. Apparently as useless as a "fifth wheel."

If the pointers in that brass director worked as usual, pointing out the direction they should go, of what possible use the compass? If, however, that brass director was a *land machine* and would not work upon salt water, how did Nephi find out the directions he must go to reach the desired promised land. He had never been there, never met one who had been there, how then did he know *which way to work his compass?* And when the naughty compass refused to work for the brothers, *how* did they find out that they were *going backwards* during the four days of storm? And if they did know without the aid of the compass that they were going backwards, what was the use of the compass? And why did they not shift their sails and go the other way? And when finally Nephi took the compass "and it did work *whither I desired it,*" not controlled, as the modern compass, by the earth's currents, but by the sweet will of Nephi, we ask again, what use the compass?*

---

*About as useful as the pioneer hog scales of California. A wide plank is balanced across a log, the hog fastened to one end, and stones piled on the other end till they balance the hog; *and then guess at the weight of the stones.*

e. I had reserved for the last what is evidently our author's great "master-piece" in the way of astounding miracles. But I have already exhausted your patience by the extreme length of this service, and I will, therefore, only in the briefest possible manner, allude to this climax of all the miracles, which occupies four or five pages of very closely printed matter in the Book of Mormon, and gathers into it more that is strange and unaccountable and foolish and physically impossible, I may safely say, than any other miracle ever performed upon earth. The author, evidently, mounts the fiery steed of his imagination and herds together every strange thing, every wonderful thing, every blood-curdling story, and every impossible thing he had ever heard of, or thought of, or dreamed of, and attempts, in this one master effort, to combine them all into one *huge miracle!*

He finds the fitting occasion for such a display of exalted genius in the death of our Lord Jesus Christ, the central point in this world's history; in fact, the central act in the grander drama of the entire universe of worlds.

In the New Testament record, we learn that while the Lord Jesus was suspended upon the cross, from the sixth hour to the ninth hour, there was darkness over all the land, that is, the land of Judea. This darkness was followed by an earthquake, the rending of the veil in the temple, etc., at the instant Jesus expired upon the cross, as if nature were expressing her sympathy with her suffering and dying Creator. All instantly ceased, however, as soon as Jesus' sufferings were ended and his soul released.

But our author, true to his instincts to beat the Bible, and everything ever written by man or by the gods, begins his account by recording a three hours' storm, the most terrific and destructive ever heard of. In three hours, destruction and desolation have swept over this entire country, from the southern coasts of South America to the northern seas of this northern continent. Sixteen great and populous cities are expressly mentioned by name as completely annihilated. Some of them set on fire and burned to ashes by the terrific lightning; others sunk down into the earth, the earth opening her mouth and swallowing them up; others still, upon the sea coast, swept away by immense ocean waves; while still others were covered up in an instant by a neighboring mountain tipping over and burying them out of sight. And these sixteen are only specimens of the fearful destruction that swept over the entire country:

"And there was a great and terrible destruction in the land southward (South America), but behold, there was a more great and terrible destruction in the land northward (North America): for behold, the whole face of the land was changed, because of the tempests and the whirlwinds and the thunderings and the lightnings and the exceeding great quaking of the whole earth. * * * And many great and notable cities were sunk, and many burned, and many shook until the buildings thereof had fallen to the earth, and the inhabitants thereof were slain." Some cities remained, "but the damage thereof was exceeding great. * * * And thus the face of the whole earth became deformed."

And all this frightful destruction of human life and property, and deforming of earth, *for what?* To signalize the consumation of God's grand plan of *mercy*, of *salvation*, of *peace and good will* to men!*

But this was only the beginning of wonders. After

---

*In entire harmony and beautiful accord with the real design of Jesus' death, we learn that in Palestine, (See Matthew, 27: 52, 53), at the instant Jesus said, "It is finished," and gave up the Ghost, graves were opened, and many bodies of the saints which slept arose, etc. That is, *life, resurrection,* and not *destruction and death*, were the accompaniments of Jesus' completion of the grand work of human redemption.

three hours' of storm, then the darkness began. And such darkness!

"Thick darkness upon all the face of the land, insomuch that the inhabitants thereof could feel the vapor of darkness; and there could be no light, neither candles, neither torches, neither could there be a fire kindled with their fine and exceeding dry wood" (Friends, could God inspire such nonsense?) And this "did last for the space of three days." Meantime, "There was great mourning and howling and weeping among all the people continually. * * * And thus were the howlings of the people great and terrible."

And right in the midst of all this horrible tempest and darkness that extinguished fires, and would not allow lights to burn, and the terrible howlings of the people, the *Lord Jesus suddenly appears upon the scene!* His body, of course, was at that time peacefully sleeping in Joseph's new tomb in Palestine; but his spirit appears and speaks with the most remarkable voice that has ever been heard on earth:

"And it came to pass that there was a voice heard among all the inhabitants of the earth, upon all the face of this land ("This land," at that time, included the whole of North and South America,) crying wo, wo, wo, unto the people."

And then follows an address that occupies two pages, in which he recounts all the terrible things that have occurred, mentions the names of the various cities that have been so suddenly blotted out of existence, and tells the reason why this terrible visitation has been permitted, because of their sins, *all the while proceeding upon the supposition* that those whom he is addressing *know all the facts.* But do they? Let me read you again:

"And in one place they were heard to cry, saying, Oh, that we had repented before this great and terrible day, and then would our brethren have been spared, and they would not have been burned in that great city Zarahemla."

How did they know that the city of Zarahemla had been burned?

"And in another place they were heard to cry and mourn, saying, Oh, that we had repented before this great and terrible day, and had not killed and stoned the prophets, and cast them out (A quotation from the New Testament): then would our mothers and our fair daughters and our children have been spared, and not have been buried up in that great city Moronihah."

This is the silliest nonsense; a physical impossibility. Please recall the situation. At the very beginning of such a frightful storm, a most destructive tornado and earthquake combined, every family will rush to their cellars, or out to some place of shelter, and there remain, frightened beyond a thought of their neighbors till the fury of the storm has passed. But they have scarcely reached their hiding places when this awful darkness overtakes them, and they are buried as in a living grave for the three days! No lights are possible, they can see nothing; and as the horrible roar of the tempest, and the reeling and rocking of the earth beneath them continues, they dare not venture outside, least they be overwhelmed. They, therefore, know nothing and can know nothing of what has happened to their nearest neighbors; how much less of towns and cities that are hundreds and some of them thousands of miles apart. The telegraph wires are all down, the railroad tracks are all torn up, the telephone business as well as the daily papers have all suspended, besides, the public highways have been rendered impassable; there is, therefore, no possibility of finding out, till after the darkness passes away, that the inhabitants of that great city Zarahemla have been burned, or that a mountain has tipped over and buried that great city Moronihah and its people out of sight forever. The whole conception, as you see, is most ridiculously absurd, and so is the closing scene:

"And it came to pass that thus did the three days pass away. And it was in the morning, and the darkness dissappears from off the face of the land, and the earth did cease to tremble, and the rocks did cease to rend, and the dreadful groanings did cease, and all the tumultuous noises did pass away, and the earth did cleave together again that it stood,(?) and the mourning, and the weeping, and the wailing of the people who were spared alive did cease; and their mourning was turned into joy,* and their lamentations into the praise and thanksgiving unto the Lord Jesus Christ, their Redeemer."

My dear friends, I have spoken thus earnestly and plainly because my whole soul is moved, profoundly moved, in this matter. I believe with all my heart, I am forced by irresistable logic to believe, that the Book of Mormon is a fraud. And believing this, I ought to speak earnestly and plainly. Let me read you again the earnest, pointed words of one of your most revered leaders, Orson Pratt:

"This book must be either true or false. If true, it is one of the most important messages ever sent from God to man, affecting both the temporal and eternal interests of every people under heaven. If false, it is one of the most cunning, wicked, bold, deep-laid impositions ever palmed upon the world; calculated to deceive and ruin millions who will sincerely receive it as the word of God, and will suppose themselves securly built upon the rock of truth until they are plunged, with their families, into hopeless despair.

---

*Guess not   The first thing they did that morning was to crawl out of their hiding places, and run over to the next neighbor to learn how they fared, and send a messenger to the other part of the city where a married son or daughter lived to see whether they are dead or alive. And as all over that city they find neighbors and dear ones by the hundreds buried under fallen houses, or wedged in between broken timbers, bruised and mangled, and yet perhaps enough left of ebbing life to plead piteously for help and succor, and as the messengers begin during the day to come in from the rural districts and from the little towns adjacent, with information of the desolation and ruin everywhere prevailing, the time for real mourning begins. During the three days it has been horror and fright and unutterable suspense; now, when the real facts are ascertained, will begin the weeping and the heart wailing.

"If, after a rigid examination, it be found an imposition, it should be extensively published to the world as such. The evidence and arguments upon which the imposture was detected should be clearly and logically stated, that those who have been sincerely, yet unfortunately deceived, may perceive the nature of the deception and be reclaimed, and that those who continue to publish the delusion may be exposed and silenced."

Dear friends, this "rigid examination" has been had, and "TEKEL"—*weighed in the balance and found wanting*—has been found written over every part of this book. It's very first claim kills it beyond recovery. God doesn't do things as we do. *Perfection* marks everything he undertakes. If the Book of Mormon is the work of God, there must be no mistakes, contradictions or blunders in it. In the Bible, some blunders in style or composition, or in its statements, may be excused because it has come down to us through human channels, and is translated by fallible, imperfect man. The Book of Mormon claims to have come down to us pure from its ancient source, without any possibility of mistake from transcription, and then to have been translated by the gift and power of God. No mistakes, therefore, or contradictions or blunders of any kind are allowable. But what has been the result of our careful examination of this book?—full of blunders and mistakes and contradictions, and human imperfections from beginning to end.

The Bible, as to its style of composition, is short, pointed, comprehensive, and says more on one page than any man on earth can say in ten pages, while the Book of Mormon is the very opposite, so full of repetitions, of awkwardly expressed sentences, of useless verbiage, &c., that any writer of ordinary skill can put three of its pages into one.

The authors of the various books of the Bible are modest, never speak of themselves, usually suppress even their own names as authors. The first opening statement in the Book of Mormon contains the word "I" and "my" some sixteen times in an egotistical way.

The Bible is original, it borrowed from nothing; Book of Mormon almost wholly borrowed; a large number of its miracles and its historical incidents are borrowed from the Bible, usually worked over and embellished (?) until their beauty and simplicity are destroyed.

The Book of Mormon is modern in its conception and make-up. A large number of words and expressions are found in it wholly of modern origin, proving beyond the possibility of question that it could not have been translated from ancient plates. This was also proved by the existence of thousands of verses quoted *verbatim*, and not translated from our English version of the Bible, and proven by the unquestioned fact that there were not plates enough all told to furnish material for one-tenth part of the Book of Mormon.

The contradictions of the Book of Mormon prove it to be a fraud. It contradicts itself in ways so foolish and needless as to prove that its author either had a short memory or a very little regard for the truth. It flatly contradicts the Bible in numerous instances. Its types contradict the types of the Bible. Its statements regarding the Holy Ghost and his work flatly contradict the statements of the New Testament.

Its peculiar way of writing prophecies proves it to be a fraud.

Its large number of very strange and very silly miracles, proves it to be a fraud.

Its wilful and malicious lies prove it to be a fraud.

The angel that dictated this book has been over and over again proven to be ignorant, self-conceited, visionary; given to exageration; forgetting important matters of record, and making numberless mistakes.

The God who inspired the book did not know his own name, forgot to furnish light and ventilation for Jared's ark; proved himself as foolish and simple as a weak, over-indulgent parent in his treatment of his pet Nephi, and as unreasonable and as cruel and spiteful as a savage in his dealings with this pet's opposers.

Friends, a book that has all these serious charges proven against it cannot be from God.

And yet I am convinced many of you have honestly accepted this book as the word of God, without the means or the opportunity of a thorough examination. If the conclusions reached are correct, I have before me a company of men and women who have been deceived into the terrible sin of adding to the word of God, of placing along side of God's blessed Book, *as its rival*, the production of a wicked deceiver. With such a spectacle before me, I ought to be moved, profoundly moved, *and so had you.*

I beseech you therefor, friends, by all that is sacred and holy, by all that is precious or desirable in the Christian's hope, and by all that is terrible in the loss of the soul, that you will give yourselves earnestly and prayerfully to a careful review of this whole question; search the Scriptures daily to see whether these things are so, and give yourselves no rest until this all important question is decided, and decided for eternity.

www.ingramcontent.com/pod-product-compliance
Lightning Source LLC
Chambersburg PA
CBHW021939160426
43195CB00011B/1157